Being Disciples of Jesus
in a Dot.Com World

Being Disciples of Jesus in a Dot.Com World

A THEOLOGICAL SURVIVAL GUIDE FOR YOUTH, ADULTS, AND OTHER CONFUSED CHRISTIANS

Ted V. Foote Jr. & P. Alex Thornburg

Westminster John Knox Press
LOUISVILLE • LONDON

Scripture quotations from the New Revised Standard Version of the Bible are copyright © 1989 by the Division of Christian Education of the National Council of the Churches of Christ in the U.S.A. and are used by permission.

Scripture quotations from the Revised Standard Version of the Bible are copyright © 1946, 1952, 1971, and 1973 by the Division of Christian Education of the National Council of the Churches of Christ in the U.S.A. and are used by permission.

Book design and cover illustration by RohaniDesign.com

First edition
Published by Westminster John Knox Press
Louisville, Kentucky

This book is printed on acid-free paper that meets the American National Standards Institute Z39.48 standard. ∞

PRINTED IN THE UNITED STATES OF AMERICA

03 04 05 06 07 08 09 10 11 12 — 10 9 8 7 6 5 4 3 2

Library of Congress Cataloging-in-Publication Data

Thornburg, P. Alex, 1960–
    Being disciples of Jesus in a dot.com world : a theological survival guide for youth, adults, and other confused Christians / P. Alex Thornburg and Ted V. Foote, Jr.—1st ed.
        p. cm
    Includes bibliographical references.
    ISBN 0-664-22560-8 (alk. paper)
    1. Christian life—Presbyterian authors. I. Foote, Ted V., 1953– II. Title.
BV4501.3 .T475 2003
248.4'851—dc21

2002027048

Contents

To
Nancy, Doyle, Pat, Patty, and Bob,
And to Ted, Cherry, Ed, Buddy, Jeanne,
and unnamed others
Who have given support in different ways
and who have mentored us
in the possibilities
for being eccentric with faithfulness
by the grace of God

Preface

In the preface to our first book, *Being Presbyterian in the Bible Belt*, we noted the gratitude we owe to Robert McAfee Brown for his 1955 book, *The Bible Speaks to You*. He demonstrated, forty-five years before we attempted something similar, that it is possible to encourage older youth and adults in theological studies of Scripture that relate both to contemporary life and history.

In the two years since the publication of *Being Presbyterian*, Dr. Brown has died. We are not aware if he knew of our personal and professional indebtedness to him, given the pioneering endeavor he undertook four and a half decades before ours. Even so, we are still in his debt, as we are still indebted to family, mentors, and fellow members of the faith communities who have nurtured us, supported us, laughed, wept, and served with us since the "baby boomer" years of our births.

Deserving of additional credit and of our immeasurable gratitude are the congregations and office staff members of First Presbyterian Church of Owasso, Oklahoma, and John Calvin Presbyterian Church of Tulsa, Oklahoma, as well as our immediate respective households: spouses Teresa and Joanie, and offspring Noah and Emma, Kendall and Payton. In the weeks of writing, while our daily responsibilities have continued without compromise, they have, with patience, both endured and encouraged us. Similarly, Marilynn Lester has, with enthusiasm, graciousness, and "life wisdom," been present both to ask crucial questions when thoughts expressed in original drafts needed clarity and to fill gaps when our computer skills were lacking.

We also owe gratitude beyond what words can describe both to the editors and publishers who made *Being Presbyterian* possible and who judged this effort important enough to attempt, as well as to many readers for their responses over the past two years. Since preparations began for this second project, we have particularly benefited from feedback offered by Presbyterians of Salida, Colorado, of the unofficial "Synod of the Permian Basin" (western Texas and southeastern New Mexico), and of Austin College. Chapters 2 and 8 of this book "sprouted" from the latter's gracious invitation to deliver the 2002 Cunningham Lectures on their campus in Sherman, Texas.

Additionally, from before any time when either of us was aware of anything, we have owed God.

This volume goes further than the first. To be able to distinguish unique aspects of being Presbyterian (as in *Being Presbyterian in the Bible Belt*) is important. Equally important is to celebrate aspects of faith we share with so many others and to explore the numerous opportunities and challenges of being God's people striving to live faithfully amid the ecumenical, interfaith, and secular components of today's world. The chapters that follow attempt precisely to explore that "canyon."

As disciples of Jesus, we recognize that significant variety exists throughout the communions and the communities in which we worship, learn, serve, and live. Further variety exists in the multiple settings and contexts in which we find ourselves day by day and decade by decade. We are convinced that youth and adults are well aware of complexities in life's relationships and values. We are equally convinced that, as "church," we have not consistently assisted and equipped one another in the task of sorting through complexities of life and faith. Much too often, we oversimplify what and how we teach and learn. Quite possibly, as "church," we oversimplify because we underestimate the ability of fellow human beings to recognize multiple factors related and relevant to present-day discipleship and life in the way of Jesus.

A word of caution: Certain references and illustrations from early 2002 in the United States may be easier for the "under-thirty crowd" to recognize than for those "born and raised" before 1970. Then again, because both authors are more than forty years old, some references and illustrations may predate the "under-thirty crowd" and, therefore, will be more meaningful to those over thirty years of age.

We welcome the conversations with readers which result from the chapters that follow, and we anticipate further growth in faith for all of us, thanks to the engagement of God with God's people, unceasing from generation to generation.

Sola Gloria Dei,

P. Alex Thornburg Ted V. Foote Jr.

Pentecost 2002

Introduction

True story. A group of seminarians travel to Central America to study the church and what God is doing among Christians there. What they experience is a spiritual crisis. In place after place they see poverty they never imagined existed, encounter suffering they could not imagine existed, and view the horror of war that no one ever imagines. Seminarians who live in the safety of the first world are not used to seeing maimed and hungry orphans. They are forced to ask themselves questions they had never asked before: Where is God in this place of death and suffering? Where are you, God?

These questions become even more pointed when the seminarians enter a nondescript house in a nondescript neighborhood of San Salvador, the capital of El Salvador. This house is the home of the United Nations Human Rights office, which strived to document human rights abuses in this country in the midst of civil war. The first thing a visitor notices upon coming in is the pictures on the walls: Pictures of people who had "disappeared"; pictures of people tortured and killed and dumped along the side of the road; pictures all over the walls, covering every square inch; pictures of men and women, adults and children, mothers and fathers, sons and daughters, brothers and sisters. The pictures surround the seminarians and press in on them, overwhelming and oppressive. The innocent faces silently ask, "Where are you, God?"

The seminarians sit down with the current head of the office, who tells them of his work and the dangers he faces every day. The past director of this very same office had been gunned down by a right-wing "death squad" while driving his children to school. The current director tells of his own experiences of arrest and torture by government soldiers and the reality that one day he will become one of the pictures on the walls. As he is talking, the seminarians notice his hands covered with burns and cuts, signs of his previous tortures. They struggle with the question that has haunted them throughout the trip: Where are you, God?

Where *is* God? The twenty-first-century world poses that question for us today more than any other. Not, Is there a God? Questions about the existence of God have run their course in the philosophical and scientific circles with neither side convincing the other, a debate that served as an interesting intellectual experiment yet never really touched the hearts of most of us. In the twenty-first century, we have less a search for an empirical proof of God's existence than a quixotic quest for God amidst the chaos and challenges of the twenty-first century. The question for this postmodern world (more on what that means later) is more a question of where God may be hiding among the joys and horrors, the traditions and fads, the hectic and messy reality we live in today. The question is not easy to answer, particularly in our culture. Part of the problem in what is called postmodernity is that a plethora of answers to where we might find God are available. The answers range from apocalyptic predictions to meditation techniques, from traditional churches to new-age mysticism, from the all-pervasive medium of television to the power of the free market. Our struggle is to discern God's voice and presence amidst the cacophony of many voices. Undertaking this quest is not easy.

A THEOLOGICAL SURVIVAL GUIDE

In our previous book together,[1] we attempted to help Presbyterians articulate their faith in conversation with a dominant strand of the Christian faith found in parts of the United States characterized as the Bible Belt. The questions posed by "Bible Belt" brothers and sisters to those of "less fundamentalist," "less neo-evangelical" perspectives are helpful so that we might better understand the biblical and theological points of view that we hold in common and those that we do not. We are grateful that many found fodder for their own thinking and questioning. In this book, we are attempting to help Christians think about their faith in light of the culture in which we reside. (Yes, North America has a culture all its own!) The questions posed by our culture are as confusing, troubling, and wide reaching for youth and other confused Christians as are the questions asked by fundamentalist, neo-evangelical Christians. Our opinion is that the two are not unrelated. Fundamentalism, megachurches, and biblical inerrancy grew out of premodernism and modernism and are a reaction to postmodernism. Though not often thought of in precisely this way, all three are interrelated (a postmodern thought!).

In this book, we desire to broaden the conversation. We hope to address questions posed by our culture in general, but also to address questions posed by Christians in general rather than limiting the conversation's scope to the part of the church called Presbyterian. You will find we speak from a Reformed perspective and understanding (different from Lutheran, Roman Catholic, Orthodox, Baptist, etc.), but we believe that in speaking from a specific context, we can address still larger questions. We are proud of the Reformed tradition and believe its theological ideas are helpful in finding God in our postmodern world. Our hope is that in broadening the circle of conversation to the more general question of being a follower of Jesus, we have something to contribute.

We believe that a postmodern time has challenges and gifts for us in the church. The challenges are difficult ones as we wrestle with hyperindividualism, rampant consumerism, and relativism. The time in which we live presents formidable obstacles to living the faith and walking the Way, but we also believe postmodernism has gifts as well. We have opportunities to look at our faith with new eyes and to deepen our understanding of what it means to be disciples of Jesus Christ.

LIVING WITH THE QUESTIONS

In this book, as in the previous one, we are not attempting to provide final answers to our questions, but rather framing the questions in a theological way. A message attributed to Max Dupree that hangs in a church office reads: "We do not grow by knowing all the answers, but by living with the questions." Christians of all stripes can place that statement in their hearts. The key to finding God is less in an answer and more in asking the right questions. We hope this book raises more questions than answers.

We also believe that theological reflection is the work of every Christian. God calls us to think and ask and struggle and follow a way of life that takes seriously questions of meaning and mystery. Theological reflection occurs in the everyday life of a Christian, informing our choices and activities, shaping our morality and political choices, and forming the meaning we make in life. In the book, we try to frame these questions by using examples from everyday life. Theology is not an ivory-tower exercise of particularly gifted thinkers. Great theologians wrestle with these questions every day, but the task of every Christian is also to struggle with them. We hope you will recognize the world we describe and its assumptions in your life and community. You may need to use your imagination to sort through these "assumptions of the world." (Think of the "Garden of Eden" story in Genesis

3. The serpent's role helps us consider "temptations," but we need to employ imagination to "let" the serpent speak.) Theology is a work of imagination in conversation with social and historical realities. As you will see, this imagination is far more real than the reality we assume exists.

Thinking concretely is important for living the faith but would be incomplete if our thinking did not also impact our practices of faith. Reflection and action are intimately related, and both must be part of every Christian's life. Being a disciple is not a spectator sport. We hope you will reflect on your own practices as individuals and communities in light of this theological task. Does your faith community reflect the strange reality called the kingdom of God, or does your community operate on the assumptions of our culture?

THE STRANGE NEW WORLD

During the twentieth century, Karl Barth[2] and others wrote and taught that we too often use the Bible as a book of answers to specific questions. That approach is not, they point out, the most appropriate way to embrace Scripture. In fact, Scripture invites readers and students to enter a strange new world where our assumptions and answers are turned upside-down by a God who doesn't act in the way we expect or even might desire. To use the Bible as a manual for certain questions of morality and life choices is to fail to truly enter its weird landscape, which offers encounters with a God of grace.

We strive to help you explore this strange new world as we tackle the dilemmas of living in a postmodern world. Too often people use Scripture as a crutch to avoid wrestling with certain questions. In the process we may dismiss other viewpoints because they do not fit our own interpretation of the Bible. We believe the Bible to be at the core of all theological questions, for "we do not read the Bible as much as it reads us."[3] We attempt to bring alive this strange new world of the Bible not necessarily to answer a particular question but to be the best place to explore the question. We hope that as you read this book, your Bible is open so you can read the stories, insights, and hopes of this amazing gift from God.

FOLLOWING JESUS IN A DOT.COM WORLD

We are fully aware of the baggage attached to the word "postmodern," not the least of which is that it can mean anything (and often does)! For this reason, we prefer to use the concept of a "dot.com world." The Internet serves as a good metaphor for our seeking God in a postmodern world. On the Internet, we have an abundance of information at our fingertips, a confusing myriad of answers to life's questions. The problem is not the lack of answers, but the task is sifting through the dross to find the helpful wisdom for our journey. The complexity and preponderance of information is so overwhelming, we despair of finding our way through the maze.

If you have searched the Web, you know the difficulty of finding what you need. You first must frame the right question in order to find the place on the Internet that is most helpful. We use search engines to aid us in our task. Picking the best search engine can be the most valuable tool for finding what we need. Without the proper search engine and the right indicators, becoming lost in the sea of Internet answers is easy to do.

The Christian tradition is a very good search engine (our "Google," so to speak) in "surfing the Web" of life for finding God. This tradition has life and form through an accumulation of people searching for God across the ages and seeking a living conversation among people who strive together as a community of faith. The Christian tradition provides a good way for filtering out the faddish and the foolish, helping us discern the "pearls of great price." Tradition is far from a dead, empty, and dry shell. It is alive, full-bodied, and organic in its encounter with the world around us. We believe our tradition is essential for us to find God in the chaos of our hyped-up and plugged-in world.

We also narrow our questions by using certain essential indicators in order to help us discern God's presence in the dot.com world. Before we begin our search on the Internet, in the first chapter we unpack the "ethos" of a postmodern world and the characteristics, assumptions, and underlying viewpoints that shape our so-called reality. In the second chapter, we explore the relationship between the church and the larger culture in which it finds itself. In particular, we define the most helpful expression of church as being eccentric. In chapter 3, we refer in detail to the great gift of God, which (we believe) is grace. We wrestle with the question of salvation in our hypercapitalistic world and how the language of market and finance shapes our understanding of God, yet erroneously.

In chapter 4, the first of four indicators for discerning God's presence is identified: humility, particularly in an "in-your-face" culture. Chapter 5 explores gratitude as a second indicator of God's presence in the world, particularly when gratitude is so lacking in our dot.com culture. In chapter 6, we look at the impact of the extreme individualism that permeates our world and how our language of community (community being the third "essential indicator of grace") needs to be expanded. Chapter 7 underscores the challenge of courage—the fourth essential indicator—as an important and vital way of being a disciple in today's world. Chapter 8 attempts to tie this gift of God's grace and the four essential indicators into a deeper understanding of hermeneutics and ecclesiology. (Don't be afraid, these big words just refer to reading Scripture and understanding the church.) By God's gift of grace and the essential indicators of grace, humility, gratitude, community, and courage, we outline a way of seeking God in chaos of the dot.com world.

GRACE AGAIN!

People who have read our previous book may recognize a similar thread running throughout our theological exploration. We understand the Reformed faith to be infused with an understanding of grace that permeates our understanding of God and God's presence in the world. This grace is God's mysterious incarnation and gift of self to a hurting world in the person and life of Jesus the Christ. Grace is not earned by us nor was it required of God. The amazing and oftentimes awkward nature of God is to love unconditionally the whole world, including us undeserving and confused human beings. Grace more than any other word describes God's engagement with our world throughout its existence; so grace is the lens we use to explore our questions.

Out of grace, certain characteristics of living as a disciple are born. These four essential indicators are not simply pulled out of the air, but are natural and biblical results of God's gift. Understanding God's love as such a gift brings humility because we cannot claim our religious life as any work of our own hands. Gratitude is a right and proper response to an unearned gift. Further, God calls us into community, through which the gift of grace is imparted. Courage is the other indicator of grace in the situations and opportunities for serving God in the world. Such a gift and indicators describe a way of following Jesus not only in the Bible Belt but in our living the faith in this postmodern and dot.com world.

LA LUCHA

"Where are you, God?" Those disciples of Jesus asked themselves this question over and over again as they listened to this man describe his work in documenting the human rights abuses in his country. "Where are you, God?" They struggled with this question as they heard him tell of his own torture and saw his hands scarred and burned as a testament to that torture. Finally one of them asked aloud, how could he do what he was doing, knowing a death sentence hung over his head? How could he have hope in this place and believe in the midst of injustice and violence? The man simply looked at them all and said, "*La lucha. La lucha.*" The struggle. The struggle.

In that moment, the visitors were able to see. In that nondescript house with its cruel pictures on the walls, they saw God. In the scarred hands and the light of hope in this man's eyes, they saw Jesus and they knew. God was there all along in the people they had met and in their struggle to witness in the midst of suffering and hunger. God was hidden in plain sight. They just had to embrace the struggle.

As we begin our journey together seeking God in a dot.com world, we wish for you the same thing. *La lucha.*

Is Postmodernism Real,
or Are We Just Making It Up?

*"Toto, I have a feeling we're not in Kansas
anymore."*
— Dorothy, in *The Wizard of Oz* [1]

A PASSION PLAY

True story: A church in suburban America put on a passion play for their
community.[2] They hoped people would be inspired and spiritually nourished as they presented the last days of Jesus' life and his resurrection, so
they pulled out all the stops to make it as professional as possible. They
used the many skills of the good-sized congregation to build sets, and they
even had some community theater people in their church who lent their
experience and expertise. They had auditions in the congregation for the
different parts, with a college student winning the part of Jesus in part
because he was the only one with a beard.

They prepared and practiced for months to make it the most powerful
spiritual experience possible. No amount of money was spared. On Good
Friday, the night of the show, they were pleasantly surprised to have a full
house. Word had spread in the community that something special was
about to happen. Little did they know how special.

Everything went well during the first part of the play. The actors
brought tears to the eyes of the audience as they told of Jesus' final days as
he ate the Last Supper with his disciples, was betrayed by Judas, stood trial,
and was condemned to death. The problem occurred during the crucial

crucifixion scene, which had Jesus dramatically hanging from the cross. What the cast did not realize was that the glue that attached the rubber head of the spear to its pole had hardened to the point that the spear was no longer as flexible as they thought. One of the soldiers, played by a junior-high boy caught up in the drama of the moment, stabbed Jesus with the spear with as much gusto as possible. Jesus on the cross cried out in pain, "Oh God, I've been stabbed."

The audience was caught up in the moment and didn't sense that anything was amiss. While they had never read those exact words in the Bible, they figured it was possible that Jesus could have said them. The stage manager, however, realized something was wrong and quickly brought down the curtains. Everyone rushed to the bleeding Jesus, who had to be taken to the emergency room for a few stitches. The cast and crew gathered behind the curtain, certain that the play was ruined. But the audience, not knowing anything was wrong, politely waited for the final scenes. The cast and crew decided the play must go on for the glory of God, and so they made preparations for the final scene, the ascension of Jesus into heaven.

Jesus' understudy, a high school senior, felt he could do it since it was only a few lines. While the understudy didn't have a beard, who was to say Jesus didn't lose his facial hair when he was resurrected? So they hurriedly said a prayer and prepared for the final powerful scene, where Jesus spoke to the disciples before he ascended into the sky in dramatic fashion.

The crew had worked long and hard to make this ascension scene as realistic as possible. They had even brought in an apparatus called Peter Pan Weights. Wires were attached to the body of the actor portraying Jesus with sandbags as counterweights, which would normally gently lift "Jesus" up into the air as he ascended into heaven. It was a simple contraption that made for a powerful image as Jesus, simply by lifting his heels, floated up into the sky. What no one had thought of was that the "new" Jesus weighed about thirty pounds less than the old Jesus. So when the final scene came to a head, as the new Jesus lifted his heels right on cue as he pronounced to the disciples that he would return, he was jerked up into the air with a shriek, disappeared into the rafters rather forcefully, and hit his head on the ceiling with a loud bang. For the second time that night, Jesus had to be taken to the hospital. But all the audience heard and saw was Jesus being yanked up into the heavens, a loud crash, and two sandals gently floating to the stage before the shocked disciples.

In a world influenced by such a variety of dynamics, many people think a hurting Jesus needs to be rushed to the hospital. Some people believe Jesus has no efficacy for today's world, and some think the church has failed to present a relevant Jesus to the questions that postmodernism poses. Is Jesus headed to the emergency room or is something else going? If Jesus is not in the hospital, where exactly is he?

Wouldn't it have been great if two sandals had been left behind, something concrete to point to? We might have the sandals in the Smithsonian Institution or in Vatican City where all could see them, as proof he existed. We could go to those sandals and bow down to them and say, look, Jesus was here and this footwear proves our case. Instead we are left like the disciples on that Ascension Day with the mystery of a Christ who is less concretely present. Like the disciples and every other generation of followers, we too must find ways to point to his presence without benefit of sandals.

This problem particularly holds for Christians who live in a world and time that some call "postmodern." The world today is a very different one from the first century, with a different set of questions to address. Some people would say that our ways of seeing the world are dissimilar and more complex, and our ways of being in the world are experienced differently. Our task, though, is the same: to witness to the one who is God with us.

Dorothy had it right. We are not in Kansas anymore. While we puzzle over what postmodernism means, we have begun to realize that faithful discipleship must take seriously the context, questions, and assertions of an unfamiliar world. Without the aid of sandals for "show and tell," we shall attempt to clarify the meaning of being a disciple in a postmodern world.

THIS IS YOUR BRAIN ON POSTMODERNISM

In the atrium of the library, Holly saw Drew sitting in a chair in front of a table piled with books and magazines and papers. Drew was sitting with his head back, legs and feet extended, hands clasped behind his head, eyes staring straight up at the ceiling.

"If you think too hard, it can hurt your head," she said as she sat down next to him.

All that came from Drew was a grunt as his gaze continued heavenward, as if he was counting pinholes in the ceiling tiles.

"Really, thinking that hard and deep can be hazardous to your health," Holly joked as she began to look at the books on the table.

"I'm just resting and letting my brain download from all this stuff."

"That shouldn't take too long, considering the small amount of data your brain can contain. So what has got your tiny computer brain all locked up?"

Drew groaned again. "I'm supposed to write a paper for my Integrative Studies course about postmodernism."

"Postmodernism? What's that? It sounds like some made-up word college professors in ivory towers invent in order to torture their students. Doesn't modernism simply mean like now, you know, kind of contemporary? So postmodernism might mean after now. Or post–present moment. Like I will go to the local pub postmodern." Holly smiled.

Again Drew groaned as he sat up and looked at Holly with bleary eyes. Gesturing toward the books all over the table in front of him, he said, "I wish I was going to the pub. But as best I can tell, there are some scholars who think that we have entered a new era in our worldview: a new time where some of the old assumptions about how to understand the world no longer apply. Then there are those who say postmodernism is simply a transition to another time that has not yet arrived. It is only an interim time until the new is born. There are even many who argue that postmodernism is nothing new. It is simply a playing out of modernism: a kind of modernism on speed. All this makes my head hurt, Holly, and I feel like my brain is a train heading out of the station."

"Or bats abandoning the belfry."

"Whatever!" Drew laughed. "If this brain wants to get out of school, I better get back to work. Thanks for stopping by. I'll let you know how it goes."

"Good luck," Holly said as she stood up from the chair. "Let me know if this postmodernism is for real or just made up."

IS POSTMODERNISM REAL? DO WE EVEN CARE?

Drew wrestles with that question in his research paper. The disciples of Jesus in the twenty-first century experience the same struggle. Many well-intentioned and thoughtful Christians do not see the efficacy of coming to terms with a concept that seems out of touch with the everyday life of the follower of Christ. Postmodernism is something about which theologians and scholars at Princeton, Harvard, and elsewhere might argue endlessly in a "foreign" language only they can understand. What does it have to do with being a disciple in Tushka, Oklahoma, or Cut N Shoot, Texas, or Toadsucker, Arkansas? (Yes, these places are real, and yes, Christians really live there.)

For a number of reasons, besides using big words and messing with our readers' heads, we two authors think that understanding postmodernism is important. One reason is that every generation of disciples seeks to speak the good news in a relevant way to and in the world. Every missionary knows that, when encountering a foreign culture, they must learn the language and customs in order to connect the gospel to that world. If we become irrelevant, we go the way of the black-and-white TV, eight-track cartridges, or big (really big) floppy disks. (If you don't know what these are, just ask an old person: someone over forty!)

Another reason is a biblical one. Jesus commanded his disciples to be not of the world but in it (John 17:16, 18), which means that his disciples were called to engage the world but not necessarily to be shaped by it. So if we do not understand the cultural trends and worldview that influence us, how then are we to resist its subtle power over us? How, too, are we able to see the ways in which the gospel challenges the world's assumptions? The result of failing to wrestle with questions about postmodernism is that we reverse Jesus' commandment. Some have observed, "We have become of the world but not really in it."[3]

In our point of view, postmodernism harbors pitfalls and dangers for living out the faith, but we also believe that much in this worldview can deepen our understanding of discipleship. The postmodern worldview does have some gifts for the disciple. Was it St. Augustine who once wrote that God is always giving us good gifts, but our hands are too full to receive them? Part of the reason for wrestling with the idea of postmodernism is so we can free our hands enough to receive God's gifts in postmodernism.

Disciples of Jesus in the twenty-first century should care about understanding postmodernism, for only in understanding it can we begin to seek God in the midst of it. One of the truths of the incarnation is that God is not simply outside history, but God's spirit can be seen in the chaos of human struggle for meaning and truth in history. We just need to know what to look for. We may be surprised at what or who is looking right back at us.

WHAT'S THE WATER WE SWIM IN?

A story is told of a river where a salmon bumped into a trout. The salmon excitedly told the trout, "Something amazing has just happened. I was swimming up the river when I jumped out of the water, and for the first time saw a far different world around me. There were tall things that were green and brown, and creatures that moved in strange ways, and all kinds of strange sights. It was incredible."

The trout seemed puzzled and could only respond with a question: "What is water?"

What is the water in which we swim? Are we even aware of it? Do we see the currents that flow around us, or do we simply assume a certain reality that nothing else can exist because that reality is the way the world works? Part of the difficulty of contemplating the concept of postmodernism is that we are asked (in a way) to jump out of the water we assumed was the real world and glimpse something else entirely. To make this leap we must be willing to look at the water where we naturally swim.

We might think of the water as the ethos or worldview of our culture. In sociology, ethos is the "fundamental character or spirit of a culture" that includes "the underlying sentiment that informs the beliefs, customs, or practices of a group or society." In dramatic literature, the ethos is the moral element that determines how a character may act rather than simply an individual's thoughts or emotion determining that action.[4] People, groups, and communities have an orientation or disposition to see the world a certain way, and to act in a particular way influenced by that fundamental character of our culture. In other words, we go where the current leads us. (Have we lost you yet? Hold on, the white water is still ahead!)

Another way of seeing the water is to look at the rivers where human beings have swum in the past. We could call one worldview *premodern*. This term describes ways of thinking and living in relation to culture, society, science, religion, etc., in which individuals are at the mercy of authority based simply on tradition. The earth was made in seven days because the Bible said so. The earth is at the center of the universe because the church said so. Women shall be subservient because God said so. A premodern way of thinking and seeing assumes truth is found in a particular tradition interpreted by a particular authority.

A premodernist sees a chair and knows it is a chair because one has always been taught that you call it a chair. The chair is a chair.

Another worldview would be modernism or the period of modernism known as modernity. Modernity describes a way of thinking and living in relation to culture, society, science, religion, etc., that began in Europe during the 1400s, 1500s, and 1600s. Some describe modernism's birth in the years of this period as "the Renaissance evolving to the Enlightenment."[5] Modernism is known for intertwining rational argument and proof with the quest for experience. Knowledge, which is scientific and objective, and its partner reason are goals worthy of increasing and pursuing. Modernism holds no authoritarian restrictions, but instead knowledge, reason, and rationality determine what is legitimate in the realms of nature and experience. We can know reality and its underlying laws because we can observe and analyze them.

A modernist sees a chair and through experimentation, examination, and reasoning discovers that the chair is made up of tiny bits of matter called atoms, orderly organized into a certain usable form with a function.

We call it a chair, yet the piece is more than a chair. The chair is made of smaller uniform components as well.

Postmodernism is a different animal entirely, challenging the assumptions of authority based simply on tradition and questioning the assumptions of rational proof and experimentation. On the one hand, postmodernism is suspicious of truth as a means of power for one particular group, such as in premodern thinking, and calls into question the uniformity and sterility of truth that modernist viewpoints espouse. Theologian Stanley Grenz argues that the ethos of postmodernism is evident today in the fields of architecture, art, theater, fiction, films, rock music, and clothing. Instead of the modernistic uniformity, postmodernism allows, encourages, and blesses irony, diversity, and disparate, nontraditional elements.[6] Postmodernism embraces diversity and questions uniformity, and it blurs the lines and distinctions between things and ideas. Postmodernism is "an ethos without clearly visible boundaries."[7] Postmodernism, therefore, calls into question basic assumptions about the world in which we live. "Toto, we really are not in Kansas anymore!"

A postmodernist sees a chair and much, much more. The postmodernist sees the world in much the same way her cousin quantum physics does. Though the chair is made up of particles even smaller than atoms, in reality, more space resides between

Say you enter a downtown high-rise building to conduct some business. As you come into the foyer of the building, you hear over the speakers a Beethoven concerto. As you enter the elevator and the door closes, you begin to notice over those speakers "Raindrops Keep Falling on My Head." As you leave the elevators and come to the receptionist desk, you hear on the speaker system a jazz riff from Miles Davis. As you pass an office to go to the appropriate place for your meeting, you hear on someone's radio the Rolling Stones. This experience is postmodern, as postmodernism does not assume (and even rejects the notion) that any single appropriate form, style, answer, or authority can claim what is legitimate or what is not. In postmodernism, you are as likely to encounter an appreciation of Gregorian chant as you are of rap.

the tiny stuff than there is stuff itself. In other words, when postmodernists encounter a chair, they would say the chair is more space than "chair."

Are you confused yet? Welcome to the postmodern worldview. Premodernism understood reality according to a particular tradition articulated by a particular authority. Reality is safe, ordered, and trustworthy. You know how the world works because God, the pope, the king, the preacher, the boss, the college professor, or your parent has told you what is real. In modernism, rationality and experimentation provide the tools for explaining reality. Laws underlie how things work in the world and provide a way for us to understand the order of the cosmos. What is real can be seen and touched and explained, at least experimentally, in logical ways.

Postmodernism instead argues that these ways of seeing the world are inadequate for explaining our current reality. We live in a multicultural, relativistic, technological, and mostly confusing world that is different even from the world where our parents grew up. Within the past fifty years the world has become smaller, with television and the Internet connecting us to places and ideas very different from our own. On Main Street you are as likely to see a synagogue or mosque as a church. We are exploring the deepest recesses of space where we might be catching glimpses of the beginnings of the universe, and we are delving into the mysteries of the tiny genes that shape our existence. The premodern vision of reality relies too simplistically on authority. The modernist vision of reality insists too much on a uniform set of scientific explanations. Both of these fail to grasp the revolutionary new age we live in today. Disciples of Jesus in a postmodern world must grapple with this new reality.

"I KNOW IT WHEN I SEE IT!"

In the late 1960s and early 1970s, the U.S. Supreme Court heard certain cases related to the subjects of pornography and free speech. In a famous quip, Justice Potter Stewart said, "I shall not today attempt further to define [pornography] . . . But I know it when I see it."

In much the same way, postmodernism may be inherently difficult to define, but you know it when you see it. Certain characteristics that we might label "postmodern" might help us identify what we are actually dealing with in this strange new world.

1. In a postmodern world, everything has a price. One characteristic of postmodernism is a hyperconsumerism whereby everything in life has a price. We attach a kind of market value to all aspects of our lives, from how we spend our time (time is money) to our worth as human beings (who is assumed more valuable: a CEO or homeless man?). A trend has even emerged to apply this kind of cost analysis to measure the success of a church. In today's world, the market exchange defines our lives, our relationships, and our self-worth.

2. In a postmodern world, the one supersedes the many. One characteristic of postmodernism is a form of hyperindividualism whereby the individual and one's needs predominate over the community. In fact, we have lost the language of community as we define relationships, marriage, family, and even the larger world according to what they can do for the individual. Even in the church, individualism reigns supreme. What does this church do for me? What programs and activities meet my needs? If you don't make me happy, I will leave! The individual measures the world according to one's own needs and responds to the world accordingly.

3. In a postmodern world, truth is relative. A characteristic of postmodernism is a suspicion of total claims to truth. In fact, truth is a matter of discussion and debate. In the infamous O. J. Simpson murder trial in the mid-1990s, two opposing truths were proclaimed, one by the defense and another by the prosecution. In one claim to truth, O. J. was the victim of an overzealous, racist police force. In the other, O. J. was a cold-blooded killer. The "truth" was decided by a jury of peers who made their decision based on the efficacy of the arguments. Perhaps they also made this decision based on their respective life experiences, as every jury does. The postmodern world is a complex and confusing collage of truth claims by various communities, some of which are directly opposed to each other. The church finds itself proclaiming a truth amid many claims to truth. This struggle is particularly difficult for the community of Jesus' disciples.

4. In a postmodern world, reality may not be real. A characteristic of the postmodern world is a confusion between what is real and what is a simulation of reality. In this age where television shapes our perception of the real world, we find it difficult to discern if it is live or if it is Memorex. Is the five o'clock news presenting reality as it is or is the broadcast an interpretation of that reality? Then comes along Reality TV, a popular new form of television that mixes real life with a scripted presentation of reality. The postmodern world challenges our assumptions about what is real and what is unreal.

5. In a postmodern world, discrete boundaries are blurring. In the postmodern world, lines between different areas of society are disappearing. No longer do we have sports and entertainment, but we have sports-entertainment. Then you have the boundaries between news and entertainment, once considered very separate, becoming more blurred as news has become a form of entertainment and entertainment a central part of the news. (Think of the circus surrounding the O. J. Simpson trial.) The church too finds itself blurring those lines between church as entertainment and the church as a political party. Part of the challenge and difficulty of making our way as disciples in a postmodern world is this lack of clarity in a borderless society.

IT'S HERE WHETHER YOU LIKE IT OR NOT!

Postmodernism is more than a difference in styles, although stylistic differences are part of the postmodern ethos. Even from a more modernist perspective (scientific and objective), differences have always existed, in opinions, methods, styles, and customs. For example, clothing worn in arctic regions differs from clothing worn in equatorial regions. Also, at a given gathering of a religious community, some people may be wearing expensive designer clothing and others wearing secondhand clothing. Some early twenty-first-century church-watchers have even said the most emotional arguments in Christian congregations are frequently arguments over style of music in worship. Will it be traditional or contemporary? (Historians will point out that these arguments existed long before the present time.)

One school of thought in the church would simply use the stylistic differences that are part of postmodernism. People with this way of thinking pay close attention to sociological trends and successful techniques because they are convinced that being attuned to styles and trends will help attract (and keep?) new adherents and members. The postmodern world is engaged only at a superficial level in an attempt to benefit from contemporary fads. Another school of thought would retreat from the encroachments of the postmodern world by circling the wagons of orthodoxy against "the barbarians at the gate." People in this school do not engage the postmodern world at all. Both groups actually tolerate little if any discussion of postmodern elements influencing theology, faith, or discipleship.

Disciples of Jesus in the twenty-first century cannot swallow whole the elements of the postmodern ethos nor uncritically adopt postmodern elements. We also cannot avoid the postmodern world in which we live. We all now, so to speak, wear postmodern clothes. The challenge is creating a conversation between our tradition or story and the postmodern world in which we swim. In the process of critically studying traditions and cultures shaping us, we are reformed over and over by God's spirit both among God's people and in the world. We are not reformed by authoritarian teachings, uncritical conformity, or anarchic relativism, but by God's spirit alive preeminently in Jesus of Nazareth, whom his disciples called "Lord."

WILL YOUR FOUNDATION CRACK?

In several parts of the United States during the twentieth century, many houses were built with concrete slab foundations, which was (and still is) thought by many to be the best sort of foundation. At times, though, the advocates of concrete slabs did not know or did not communicate the downside of such slabs. If the geographic area suffers a prolonged drought and the ground beneath and around the slab contracts as it dries up, the slab can crack, and the structure built upon it can slip and crack also. Faith too can crack if it is rigid like a concrete slab.

What if we saw the church as a boat sailing on the waters of the world? That's actually a very old image of the church. What if this boat is tossed to and fro by waves that no one can control? The wind (spirit) in the sail gives the boat some sense of direction, but the wind blows where it will and the boat must sail where the wind goes. Some fear and anxiety occur as one sails on the vastness of the ocean, but the boat sails on.

A few weeks after the September 11, 2001, terrorist attacks in the northeastern United States, a high school student named Laura wrote the following, which was printed in her church newsletter.

> Immediately, many people's reaction to this incident (including mine) was fear. Fear of what? Fear of many things: our lives, our family's lives, our country, the end of the world. All these things are natural reactions. . . . Throughout the next two weeks, I was "hit" several times with a greater fear. That fear came from the message that my friends who are not Christians were going to hell. One of my friends stood up and said, "We need to save those people in our school who are not Christians because they are the ones that are going to hell." . . . I was so upset I started to become angry with God. . . . Then my Dad gave me a book where I learned . . . that we should not live in fear, but in gratitude, love, and celebrating the wonderful grace of God that we have experienced. . . . I believe we should go out and share the grace of God with those who don't know God's grace, love, and mercy. We should also live in gratitude and not in fear, or in judgment of others, or in fear of our own afterlife. . . . I hope that all of us will be more graceful and less judgmental.[8]

Laura's faith foundation was a slab cracking under the drought of her anxiety. She was afraid (as we all were) given the vastness of the waves of terror and unpredictability that can toss us around in this world. She sought other possibilities for understanding her crisis of faith, possibilities about which her friends could not see from their own perspective of literalistic Bible reading and uncritical acceptance of religiously reinforced authoritarian teaching. According to her, the gift of grace found in her own tradition opened other possibilities, which were gifts as well.

God's grace that we know so completely in Jesus of Nazareth can heal the cracked foundations of human lives. We can discover the gifts of God present even in the midst of the confusing, complex, and scary world we call postmodern.

NOTES AND JOURNALING OPPORTUNITIES

I.   Parts of this chapter with which I have mostly agreed in the past:

II. Parts of this chapter with which I have mostly disagreed in the past:

III. Parts of this chapter which have presented new thoughts or information for me:

IV. What's in this chapter . . .

(a) prompts me to remember

(b) prompts me, from years past, to wonder about

(c) prompts me to want to ask, to investigate, to research

(d) prompts me to wonder about changing

(e) prompts me to wonder about the near future in the following ways

(f) prompts me to wonder about the more distant future in the following ways

V. Personal writings, sketches, drawings related to this chapter

Is God Eccentric or Comfortably Middle Class?

> *"Can we be Christians and middle class?"*
> —John Nelsen[1]

> *"They do not belong to the world . . . (yet) I have sent them into the world . . . so that the world may believe that you have sent me."*
> —Jesus praying (John 17:16, 18, 21)

That Germany, a country famous for its music, intellectual vigor, and academic disciplines, could fall prey to the Nazis' "final solution"—which saw millions of Jews, gypsies, and others killed in concentration camps—has always been somewhat of an enigma. One question in particular is the German church's role in the midst of this genocide, and the church's failures to resist in any significant way and to respond to this crisis of the human soul. These failures are particularly horrific in part because so many of the great biblical and theological minds of that time were in Germany, yet the resistance to the Holocaust was so meager as to be almost nonexistent. That theological problem is particularly thorny for the church after the Holocaust. In the twenty-first century, we cannot think theologically unless we understand and resist those forces that shaped the church's failure to respond to one of the greatest tragedies of history.

While much has been written on the Holocaust, Daniel Jonah Goldhagen has done a rather remarkable thing in his landmark book, *Hitler's Willing Executioners: Ordinary Germans and The Holocaust*.[2] Goldhagen has proposed a new idea in Holocaust studies that throws conventional wisdom on its ear. In the study of the Holocaust and the Germans' capitulation to the Nazi plan, two camps of thought have prevailed. In one, the theories propose that ordinary Germans were duped into the final solution, that the planned execution and murder of so many Jews went incremental step by incremental step until the Germans were too far along the road to turn back. Ordinary people were just unaware of what was going on until it was too late. The second theory about ordinary people's lack of resistance holds that they were frightened into following orders and through intimidation forced to follow along with the persecution and execution of so many Jews. The Nazi machine was simply too big and overwhelming for the German citizen to resist, and the only path of survival was to acquiesce and close one's eyes to what was happening. These two overarching themes have driven much of the exploration of Holocaust studies and our explanation for how such a terrible practice can occur in a civilized society.

Goldhagen articulates a theory that calls these two explanations into question. His thesis is that a rampant anti-Semitism, eliminationist in nature, was part and parcel of German society.[3] Tracing its roots to Christian beliefs in the Jews as the Christ killers and as inherently evil in their rejection of the Christ and later expanded into a belief of Jewishness less as a religious choice than as a racial category of people who were detrimental to society, German society incorporated an ethos that Jews and their influence must be eliminated from society. Elimination meant being deported out of the country or isolated into their own communities in ghettos, or finally killing Jewish men, women, and children. Goldhagen's argument is that for the ordinary German, this eliminationist anti-Semitism was the underlying cognitive model of their culture: Jews were an evil people who had to be removed from good society for the country to prosper. This outlook was how Germans saw the world, unquestioned and unchallenged!

So for Goldhagen, the arguments that ordinary Germans were duped fails to take into account the vastness of the Holocaust project undertaken by the Nazis, its permeation of all sectors of society, and the willingness and in fact eagerness of the populace to take part in such an endeavor. In this view Hitler did not create anti-Semitism in German society, but rather German society birthed Hitler and the Nazis and their final solution.

As to the argument that ordinary Germans were frightened to speak out and respond to this genocide occurring among them, Goldhagen argues that in a number of incidents the general population spoke out against Nazi policies and the government responded to this criticism.[4] In one case, the killing of some deemed physically and mentally defective raised such a hue and cry among the populace that the Nazis stopped this initial foray into mass executions. In another incident, when the German wives of some Jewish men protested their arrest, the Nazis relented and released the husbands. Whether these incidences of civil unrest would have ultimately stopped the Nazis in their plans for the Jewish solution is not the question, but such unrest indicates that the populace could hinder and even prevent atrocities if it was so inclined.

The frightening reality was that no public institution spoke out against treatment of the Jews and their ultimate elimination from German society. Universities, businessmen, professors, and political opposition groups all bought into the political culture, the cognitive model of the Jews as detrimental to society in general and the need for their removal.[5] The moral bankruptcy of the church is evident in its utter failure to speak out against the anti-Jewish atrocities.[6] Even more frightening is the church's full participation in the project itself, fomenting anti-Semitism in the Christian press and the complete capitulation of the church to the Nazi Party. Even the Barmen Declaration, the famous document of the Confessing Church speaking out against the Nazification of the church, was formulated by only a small minority of the Christian church. In fact, the Barmen Declaration did not address the horrors being inflicted upon the Jews but was a statement more concerned with theological and institutional concerns. The church failed in a time when it was needed the most.

This failure is particularly troubling when we see the pervasiveness of the anti-Semitic ethos even among the best biblical scholars and theological teachers of our age. Consider Gerhard Kittle, a name recognizable to any biblical scholar who uses his theological dictionary of the New Testament. Kittle spoke in 1933 of the Jewish problem and even explicitly raised the extermination solution, although he found it impractical and therefore argued for a guest status for Jews, namely a separation of Jews from the host people.[7] Even Karl Barth, the theological father of the Barmen Declaration and staunch opponent of the Nazis, had to overcome his own biases to defend Jews. This great theologian wrestled with deep anti-Semitic feelings. In an Advent sermon Barth preached in 1933, he denounced Jews as an "obstinate and evil people," yet a year later, in his December 10, 1934, sermon, he clearly declared: "Jesus Christ was a Jew."[8] This statement provoked some worshipers to walk out of the service.

The evidence is overwhelming that ordinary German Christians did not resist but in fact participated in the horrific acts of cruelty and killing that characterized the Holocaust. They held a belief, a cognitive model of the Jews, that motivated and shaped the genocide despite their theological and biblical knowledge and despite having a high sense of morality about other aspects of life. As Martin Niemoller stated in his lecture in Zurich in March 1946, "Christianity in Germany bears a greater responsibility before God than the National Socialists, the SS and the Gestapo. We ought to have recognized the Lord Jesus in the brother who suffered and was persecuted despite him being a communist or a Jew. . . . Are not we Christians much more to blame, am I not much more guilty, than many who bathed their hands in blood?"[9]

Our reason for sharing this history lesson is not to stand indignant over the failure of the church in Germany, but to illustrate the dangers of a church acculturated, a church that does not question the basic assumptions of how culture constructs our cognitive models. The challenge of history in the 1930s and 1940s in Germany is to ask ourselves as the church, What ethos shapes our worldview? What social constructs define how we understand the world? What in our own society do we take as a simple fact of existence, much as the German church took as fact the need to rid society of Jews and other undesirables?

We want to be clear that we are not arguing that anti-Semitism is necessarily a central social construct of our age, though time and again, it seems quite alive, even in the words of religious and political leaders. Our history as a church in the United States has its own ghosts to face in its cognitive models and treatment of African Americans, Native Americans, and women. The question we pose in this chapter is a far more delicate and demanding one than a simple history lesson. What social constructs go unquestioned and unchallenged by our church today? What cognitive framework do we operate out of that history will look back on and ask, "How could they have done that? How could they have believed that?"

THE COUNTERCULTURAL CHURCH?

These questions are important for obvious reasons as the church seeks to be faithful in the twenty-first century. We struggle with questions of what being "countercultural" means. Many scholars point out that the church has entered a post-Constantinian age. They are referring to the joining of the church to the state when Emperor Constantine embraced Christianity as the unifying religion of the realm. This joining has had a checkered past at best, but the modern era has seen the separation of church and state. The church in North America, while living with this idea of separation, still enjoyed a position of privilege in society, but in the twenty-first century the church finds its position in society diminished and its voice no longer assumed to shape the state. The church thus struggles with its appropriate place in society and its role in the world. Much of the angst and theological thinking in our time comes from wrestling with where the church fits in relationship to the culture.

Some people argue for a return to the "good old days" when the church had its position of power. America has always been a Christian nation, they argue, and should state so emphatically with the Ten Commandments placed in the county courthouse and prayer returned to schools. More subtle forms of this attitude of the marriage of the state to Christianity are reflected in making no distinction between being a Christian and being an American. This relationship is simply assumed, as some churches begin their worship by saying the Pledge of Allegiance and singing the national anthem. If anyone doubts the insidious attraction between church and state, then simply try to remove the American flag that sits in many of our sanctuaries. The complexity of the relationship between our allegiance to the state and allegiance to God is difficult to delineate.

Other people argue that, in this post-Constantine time, the church is called to an earlier form that is more countercultural in nature. The church finds itself in opposition to the culture and the state, challenging its more troublesome influences. In the extreme are those Christian communities supposedly supportive and connected to Timothy McVeigh's bombing of the Murrah Federal Building in Oklahoma City. Their belief is that the culture is so decadent that the only hope is to destroy those institutions that uphold it. Saner voices argue for a vision of the church as a community in the midst of a culture witnessing by its uniqueness to the larger world. The church is a colony of resident aliens,[10] a community in contrast to the society in which it exists. This particular vision of the church as countercultural is often based on Jesus' prayer indicating that disciples are to be "in the world but not of the world" (John 17:11, 14). This understanding has influenced much theological reflection as we wrestle with what the calling of being faithful in this diverse world means.

Thus we come to the crux of the meaning of being a countercultural church. In light of the church in Hitler's Germany absconding from any moral authority, the challenge is to understand and counter the forces that our Christian communities today should be resisting. The problem for the church in Germany was that, on the one hand, it saw no conflict between the gospel and the Nazification of the church; on the other hand, the church was so self-absorbed with its own institutional structures that it could not see the real face of Jesus Christ in those people whom the state was killing. Would a deeper understanding of being countercultural have made a difference?

Counterculturalism has to be more than pietistic actions of individuals in protest against a monolithic culture, more than a resistance to certain messages our media conveys, more than dressing differently or wearing one's hair in a particular shade of purple, though that is a pretty color. To be truly countercultural is to think differently, to view the world differently, and to see reality differently. For the German Christians, counterculturalism would have been to see Jesus when they saw a Jew. Counterculturalism at its best calls into question the basic assumptions of how our culture constructs the world.

But the very term "countercultural" as defined by society's cognitive models is problematic. First, when asked to consider countercultural communities, we tend to think first of the Amish or the aesthetic person who withdraws from society to join with one of their own separated communities. In so doing, these communities intend to offer a witness at odds with modern society's materialism and decadence. While much is to be admired in such communities, their withdrawal from the world implies that their goal is simply to be different and at odds with the world's values, as if that is enough. For Christians in many traditions and in particular the Reformed tradition, this goal does not apply. The call is not simply to be against culture but to be part of its transformation, to be a participant in the midst of it and therefore part of its growth and change into something more just and compassionate.

The second fallacy of the countercultural model is the assertion that one can completely escape the cultural ethos that forms our social constructions of the world. The proposition of many isolationists is that, by being part of a community against culture, one can get away from the underlying identification as defined by the culture. The problem is that no one really lives without an ethos shaped by the world around us. We cannot totally escape the surrounding culture. The countercultural movement of the hippies of the 1960s at its best exemplified peace and love, yet in many ways the hippie movement was just as indulgent, angry, and violent as the culture it claimed to be resisting. The language of being countercultural seems to imply escaping from society's values when what we do is simply import them to different communities.

The third danger is the very idea that being countercultural constructs a worldview defined on being *against* something rather than *for* a particular value or idea. The sense prevails that we find our meaning in what we resist and argue against. "We are not *them*, and therefore we are better than them. We are not those people over there," as if that tells us who we are.

This approach will always be a particular fault of the Christian church, for as long as we tend to define ourselves as "not being like those people who do such sinful things," the popular image of Christians will have less to do with what we stand for than what we oppose. For example, the negative imperatives from fundamentalist Christians have been stereotypically characterized as, "Don't dance. Don't drink. Don't smoke." We disciples of Jesus too frequently can be known more for judging and less for compassion, more for our turning away and less for our welcoming of people different from ourselves, more for our resisting spontaneous opportunities than for our joyful embracing of them.

THE ECCENTRIC CHURCH

We believe that a different metaphor is better suited for responding to the cognitive models that our society imposes. That metaphor is the idea of eccentricity. Eccentricity (or "the state of being eccentric") can be defined in several ways: as not having a common center, as oddness of behavior, and even as the distance of a revolving body from the center of the orbit. To be eccentric is to be off center, as we might describe a certain planet's or comet's eccentric orbit around the sun if that orbit is less circular and more elliptical. The planet doesn't follow a normal centric path, but, as a mass in space, has its axis or point of rotation distant from what would be a "center" of orbit. This metaphor serves as a description of the church as off center of our society and culture, not having a common center with the culture.[11] The church is a community that (at its best) simply doesn't reflect the culture it lives in, but moves off kilter within the orbit of that society by revolving around a different center point.

Eccentricity is displaying an oddness of behavior as our culture defines it. Eccentricity is acting in ways that society would describe as foolish and not conforming to conventions. When we describe someone as eccentric, we understand them to be out of the ordinary expectation of proper behavior and decorum. Each of us has probably encountered people we would describe as eccentric, and to contemplate using such a term to describe ourselves as Christians may be strange.

In a study done in Great Britain a number of years ago, Dr. David Weeks and journalist Jamie James looked at eccentricity and mental health. They examined those people who would be described as dancing to a different drummer, who in their lives exemplified behavior out of the norm. Neighbors would refer to them as odd; families would speak of them as that strange uncle or batty aunt in the family. In describing these eccentrics, the researchers wrote about people who saw the world differently and valued different things, not simply to be different, but because of their own way of seeing and valuing. Their view wasn't a rejection of the world. In fact, these people tended to be rather engaged in their strange way with other people and the institutions surrounding them. Rather, the culture simply found them eccentric and would often dismiss them because of their eccentricity.[12]

The study's results were rather interesting. These eccentric people tended to be healthier, mentally and physically. They tended to be happier and more alive. Where often their behavior didn't endear them to their neighbors and resulted in some rejection by people who were put off by eccentric behavior, the eccentrics still had a deeper sense of who they were and what they were about.[13] We can be left though with a rather disturbing question: Are the eccentrics disappearing from our world? Is one of the characteristics of our age the shaping of people into a homogenized world where eccentricity is discouraged?

What if we envisioned our faith communities as places of eccentricity, places that foster a healthy eccentricity, places that create eccentrics not for the sake of simply being different, but because we *are* different? Rather than thinking in terms of the countercultural with its problems of not engaging the world, its failure to take the world seriously, and its definition not in the positive but in the negative, eccentricity as we would define it resists these problems by articulating a different metaphor. Eccentrics are engaged in the world but embrace differences in the way they think, value, and act. Eccentrics do not deny the impact of the world upon them, but find ways to break from a monolithic culture to be different, to be who they truly are: people of God!

A rather eccentric movie of recent years that has gained a cult following, *Chocolat*,[14] tells the story of a small town in France characterized in an opening scene by a frowning statue of the founding father. This town is viewed in all grays, and the people are a faithful people who go to church and hear sermons about self-denial and the path of purgation. The movie starts at the beginning of the Lenten season, and in the mayor of the town we see the epitome of one who is faithful by denying himself things of this world, certain foods and activities. But then this strange and exotic woman comes with her daughter into this gray, drab town to open up a chocolate shop. This woman is always dressed in flamboyant clothes—red more often than not—and is always laughing, as contrasted with the frowning townspeople.

The mayor is quite aghast at this woman opening up a chocolate shop in the middle of town, especially during Lent, and comes to view her as the enemy of all that is right and moral. He tells the townspeople to avoid her shop, for she is the devil in disguise, but the woman who makes confections and candies that delight the eye and tongue begins to have some customers. One sad woman whose husband has not touched her in years comes to her shop, and the red-garbed woman sells her some chocolate-covered peppers to raise the passions. Soon the woman and her husband are back, much in love, for more chocolate peppers. A woman beaten down by life and her husband finds in the owner of the shop someone who gives her the strength and freedom to come out of her shell. An older gentleman who has secretly loved a widow finds the courage to leave little candies on her doorstep, and a romance begins to blossom. All these people's lives begin to be changed by the joy and life that surround this woman.

Soon a band of gypsies comes into town. The mayor warns the people about their sexual immorality, yet the woman invites them into her shop. Urging the young Catholic priest to denounce her in his sermon every Sunday, the mayor even begins to write the sermons himself. Everything comes to a head on the night before Easter morning when the mayor, tormented by his own desires, breaks into the chocolate shop and stuffs his face full of chocolates and candies. He passes out, only to be awoken on Easter morning by the shopowner holding a glass of seltzer water. She promises to tell no one what he had done. The priest, who has seen it all, begins his Easter service sermon by saying he is not sure what to say on this morning of resurrection. Maybe we should focus on Christ's humanness and love of life. Maybe our goodness is defined less by what we deny, by what we resist, and by who we exclude, and is measured more by what we create, what we embrace, and who we include. The closing scene of the movie is of a town come alive in colors and the joy of life in a great Easter party. The last shot is of the statue in the middle of the square, except this time the statue is smiling.

WHAT MAKES US ECCENTRIC?

What is it that we embrace as a church that would make us eccentric in our world today? What is it that we include that shapes us into eccentricity? In the next part of the book, we lift up those theological ideas, those visions of the world that would today be considered eccentric in our culture. We believe God to be particularly eccentric in a world where we define God as comfortably middle class. If Jesus is the center we revolve around—and if the vision he had of God and God's purpose is the vision shaping our lives—then we will find ourselves in an eccentric orbit. If the church in Germany in the twentieth century has any lesson for us, it is the importance of seeing our center as being very different from the assumed values and vision of our culture. We must ask ourselves what vision of the world and humanity's role in it we revolve around. We endeavor to offer some ideas on that question.

NOTES AND JOURNALING OPPORTUNITIES

I. Parts of this chapter with which I have mostly agreed in the past:

II. Parts of this chapter with which I have mostly disagreed in the past:

III. Parts of this chapter which have presented new thoughts or information for me:

IV. What's in this chapter . . .

(a) prompts me to remember

(b) prompts me, from years past, to wonder about

(c) prompts me to want to ask, to investigate, to research

(d) prompts me to wonder about changing

(e) prompts me to wonder about the near future in the following ways

(f) prompts me to wonder about the more distant future in the following ways

V. Personal writings, sketches, drawings related to this chapter

How Much Is Grace, Or Is It Just Cheap?

Grace in an eBay World

"I ain't ever known anything to be cheap that I couldn't do without having."
—An Oklahoma horseman

"My brother, you belong no longer to evil, but to good. It is your soul that I am buying for you."
—A compassionate Roman
Catholic bishop to Jean Val Jean[1]

In Victor Hugo's *Les Miserables*, the character Jean Val Jean is traveling through the French countryside in 1815 after being released from prison. He has served a sentence of close to twenty years for stealing bread to feed his sister and her children. His experience has left him embittered and angry at the world. People shy away from his bitter visage as he enters the city. According to the law of the land, he must inform the local government of his recent incarceration by presenting a yellow passport. The authorities look askance at this disheveled gentleman as he goes to search for lodging for the evening. Everywhere he goes, doors are shut in his face as word has spread that a convict is now in town. Home after home refuses him entry as they fear what he represents. The final straw comes when he seeks shelter in a dog pound, and even the dogs run him off.

Depressed and filled with rage, he comes to one more house, the home of the bishop. When Jean Val Jean knocks on the bishop's door, he is invited to come in, a very different reception than he received from all the other homes. He is invited to eat supper with the finest silverware and silver plates adorning the table. Jean Val Jean is taken aback by the hospitality of his gracious host who is well aware of his past. That evening, as everyone else sleeps, Jean Val Jean sneaks out of the house with the silver.

The next morning the bishop is eating his breakfast when the gendarmes bring Jean Val Jean back to his house. They tell the bishop that they found this criminal with the bishop's silverware. The bishop does a surprising thing at this point. He rushes to embrace Jean Val Jean and tells him he had forgotten to take the silver candlesticks when he had left. Much to the surprise of the gendarmes, he gives them to the shocked Val Jean. The bishop whispers to Val Jean that because of this act, his life is not his own and now belongs to God. From that beginning point, Jean Val Jean is a changed man. Through this simple act of grace, his life is transformed. Victor Hugo illustrates throughout the rest of the novel how Jean Val Jean lives a grace-full life.

LIVING IN A CONSUMER WORLD

Most of us, if we would admit it, find this act of the bishop more than a little shocking. His extension of grace to an undeserving Val Jean strikes us at best as gullible and at worst codependent. His gift doesn't make sense. Letting Val Jean suffer the consequences of his actions so that he may learn from his sins would seem more logical. To have the punishment fit the crime rather than letting him go, much less giving him more to take, would make more sense. This story of grace is especially puzzling for our culture's way of seeing and understanding the world.

We live in a consumerist culture that works in a predictable way: you get what you pay for and, conversely, are paid for what you earn. It is a fair-market exchange. In a consumerist world, you get what you deserve. I pay you this amount of money and I get this product; I give you a day's work and expect a day's wages. Everything has its price, and we understand that in a fair-market exchange we exchange one value for another of equal value.

The world is like one big eBay—the wildly popular Internet auction site and shop—where we can shop for anything in the world if we have the means to buy it: from cars to homes to tattoos to antiques. In marketing and business parlance, we are known as consumers, and we can buy not just products but an image or attitude: sexiness for the price of a particular car, or infinite knowledge for the price of a computer. Thus, whether we realize it or not, we operate on the assumption that life is shaped around purchasing and consuming whatever we need: food, clothes, services, or even happiness.

After the horrific events of September 11, 2001, the message to Americans on how they could support their country was to "go out and buy things. By being consumers, you can help save the economy and therefore aid the country." Many people follow the daily changes on the New York Stock Exchange with the fervor of a cult. In fact, one could say that market exchange is a new form of faith, as stocks are traded and sold simply on consumers' confidence in the system.

To call this market a free market is an oxymoron, because nothing is ever really free. Our value as a consumer is what we can pay to have what we want. People who have worked hard and earned their way are held up as paragons of our culture. Who are our cultural heroes? They are the rich and famous like Bill Gates, who earned his way to the top by dint of his drive and business acumen. They are the athletes who make millions of dollars by attaching their name and skill to a particular product. Often our own self-worth is less a psychological characteristic than the size and extent of our financial portfolio.

To better understand the dynamics that shape our consumerist worldview, we could look more deeply at the assumptions that define what we value. Do we value the work of the CEO over that of a teacher? Do we value the work of the stockbroker and dismiss the stay-at-home parent? Are most students striving in their education not necessarily for knowledge gained but for the money that could be made in their chosen occupation? We even characterize poverty as a moral failing, a character deficiency. When a person ceases to be a money earner, they are of less value to the society around them and in fact are perceived as a problem for society to solve. We cannot elude the inescapable truth that, in today's world, our primary identification and value are as consumers of material goods.

In an eBay world, even time is money. We receive bills for the use of minutes on a cell phone or computer line, and professionals charge money by the hour for the performance of their duties. We value time, we buy time, and we spend time. Life in a consumerist culture is fast paced because time is so precious. Nothing is more distasteful than wasting time in a culture when time is just another commodity on the market.

Much good has come from free-market exchange, as more goods are available to more people than at any other time in history. The dilemma is that this consumerism has infiltrated most aspects of our institutional life. The lines between economics and daily life have blurred. Marriages now have contracts that protect the assets of the particular individuals in anticipation of dissolution of the partnership (divorce!). After all, you don't want your future marriage partner to have something they didn't earn. Even in public education, students are understood as consumers; the proposals for a voucher system allow the consumer (student) to be a better shopper for the most effective school. Sports are simply no longer a pastime but a business, and the daily TV news has ties to corporations and the bottom line. The frightening truth of consumerist culture is that our daily lives are shaped and viewed according to economic principles, and even our Christian faith feels the effects.

THE CONSUMER CHURCH

Some people understand the religious life in terms of an exchange of one thing for another. Salvation is earned according to our doing the right actions or saying the right words. We exchange our holiness and morality in order to pay our way into heaven. Spirituality becomes another commodity: if we use this technique or say this prayer, we can reach enlightenment. A devotional book on the biblical prayer of Jabez, from 1 Chronicles 4:9–10, has become extremely popular.[2] The book presumes that if you ask God, then you can expand your territory and receive God's blessings.

Across the years, many preachers have claimed that if you have the right relationship with God, then God grants you personal wealth. This line of thinking originates from a certain "strand" of theology and teachings in parts of the Bible. In a consumer church, one can easily sense that faith is a means to an end, whether that end (goal) be a longer marriage, more happiness, or even greater health.

This hyperconsumerism shapes our understanding of what being a church means. The success of a church is based on what some have called three Bs (buildings, bucks, and butts). Churches are considered successful when they have big buildings, lots of money in the budget, and a lot of butts in the pews (attached to the rest of the human body). This consumer index of quantifiable and economic success reflects our fascination with finding consumers for our brand of faith.

In many ways, evangelism simply becomes another marketing tool to attract people to the services of the church. Church growth becomes a popularity contest to see which can be more attractive to the most people. How many of us have heard the phrases, "I am shopping for a church," and "The church should be run like a business"? So much of what underlies these statements is a worldview that the church and its programs exist to be consumed and purchased by a consumer. The logical conclusion is that, if a church fails to meet the needs of the consumers, they will stop giving the church their financial support. After all, we want "a good bang for our buck," especially when it comes to the church.

What would it mean to be "eccentric," given this prevailing vision of faith and church as the consumption of religious services? What theological ideas could help us resist this view of the world, which understands that even faith is a commodity bought with the right words or actions? What ideas of how God works in the world counter this consumerist vision of faith?

Let's explore the possibility that a core theological idea shapes the Christian understanding of who God is in the world and how God interacts with the world. Philip Yancey referred to it as "the last, best word."[3] Paul's standard salutation beginning his numerous letters to churches included this word. Jesus, while not often using the word explicitly, told stories describing it in many different forms. That word is "grace"!

THE PRODIGAL FATHER

Luke records in the fifteenth chapter of his Gospel (verses 11–32) a parable told by Jesus often referred to as the parable of the Prodigal Son. "Prodigal" means recklessly extravagant and lavish. Doesn't this also (and possibly better) describe the eccentric behavior of the father? Jesus begins his story with the younger son demanding his share of the property that will belong to him. This demand is more than a little scandalous for the first-century listeners of this parable, given that younger sons had no claim on any inheritance from their fathers. But the father, who should be insulted by such a demand, instead acquiesces. Soon the son is off to a distant country where he proceeds to squander his money on wild living. (We can imagine him playing craps in Las Vegas with two prostitutes at his side.) After all his money is gone, a famine hits, darn the luck. He resorts to hiring himself out to feed pigs, which is particularly offensive for a Jew to have to associate with unclean animals. The younger son has hit bottom, and, as the parable says, for a time the son is willing to eat even the slop he is feeding the pigs because no one has been willing to give him anything.

Then comes an intriguing turning point in the parable. The younger son is described as coming to his senses and realizing that his father's hired men have bread enough, when here he is dying of hunger. So why doesn't he just go to his father and tell him how sorry he is and that he is even willing to work as one of his father's hired hands? Realizing he can do exactly that, the son sets off to return to his father. Many people describe this moment in the parable as a moment of repentance, a true desire to confess one's sin and rely on the mercy of the father. We would assert, though, that the son may not be truly repenting, but simply acting out of the selfishness that has characterized his life to this point. His repentance seems a device to maneuver himself into a better and improved condition rather than representing any true desire to turn himself around.

In our consumerist culture, repentance plays a major role in Christian thought and yet, like the younger son, seems to be less about true change and more about receiving something in return. Repent, so you can be saved and enter heaven. Repent, for the end of the world is at hand, and you will be part of the remnant taken up into God's army. All these visions of repentance have, at their core, a consumerist reason for following God. Repentance, at least as understood in this context, would seem to be less about a conversion to something than paying for insurance to be saved.

Jesus continues his story with a subtle but important line. "But while he (the younger son) was still far off, his father saw him and was filled with compassion; he (the father) ran and put his arms around him and kissed him" (Luke 15:20). What is so amazing about this passage is that the father must have been searching the horizon for the son and yearning for his return, in order to see him far off in the distance. We can imagine the father waking up every morning, searching the horizon for the one who has left him. When he at last spies the son, he runs (!) not to berate or scold this son, who has left him, but to embrace and kiss this one who has returned. Notice that this reception occurs even before the son has had the chance to speak his words of repentance. The younger (foolish?) son is welcomed in compassion with a kiss and a hug.

This son finally offers his statement of repentance. We can imagine he had been practicing the line for a while as he walked along the road on the way home. But his statement of shame seems overshadowed, even ignored, as the father orders his servants to bring out a robe and put a ring on this son's finger and sandals on his feet, and kills the fatted calf to celebrate with a party. To envision a party for the wayward son who has been lost and now has been found seems simultaneously natural and strange: natural, in that the son has returned and the joy of the father is evident; strange, in that this son insulted his father, wasted away his inheritance, and returned a beggar. The son, though, is now welcomed with open arms and a celebration without out really having to say he was sorry.

Then comes the older son. He approaches the house, hears the party, and asks one of the servants what is going on. He is told his younger brother has returned and his father is throwing him a party in the joy of his safe return. At this point the older brother is angry—understandably—and refuses to go in. The father leaves the party and comes out and begins to plead with (the word implies begging and not demanding) the older son to come in and enjoy the celebration.

In response, the older brother quite righteously complains, "Listen! For all these years I have been working like a slave for you, and I have never disobeyed your command; yet you have never given me even a young goat so that I might celebrate with friends. But when this son of yours [note how the older brother subtly denies his brotherhood] came back, who has devoured your property with prostitutes, you kill the fatted calf for him!" (Luke 15:29–30). The older brother is feeling very self-righteous and does not hesitate to make his feelings known to the father, whom the son thinks is nothing but gullible.

What strikes the listener in this story is the rightness of the older son's claim. The father is not treating the older son fairly. This older son has done everything right—religiously, we might say. He has gone to church; he has given his percentage offerings (tithes); he has obeyed the Ten Commandments; and yet the party goes to the wayward son who has squandered his inheritance.

The older brother is right. This situation is not fair. Aren't you supposed to get what you pay for? A fair day's dollar for a fair day's work? And if we do well, aren't we supposed to receive the reward? In a consumer culture, of course we are!

One reason we find this parable so troubling is that the sensibilities of the older brother are also our way of seeing things. In an eBay world, as we have noted, everything has its fair price, and you are expected to receive fair value for the price you pay. The older brother has done what he is supposed to have done. He has followed the rules. He has worked hard, and he deserves the reward, the payment, for his faithfulness. This exchange makes sense to us.

But in the eccentric world of Jesus, grace doesn't work that way. Grace is extended to the undeserving, and the celebration is not simply for those who do good, but for all who are lost whom God has patiently, yet actively, awaited—watching the horizon for the opportunity to run, to embrace, and to kiss the one returning.

The next words of the prodigal father to his older son reflect this gift of love even to the self-righteous one. "Son, you are always with me, and all that is mine is yours" (Luke 15:31). In other words, the older son has received and continually receives the best gift of all: the father's presence and love that is already his and always will be his. In the "economic system" of this father's household, the older son doesn't work so he can earn something he already has received; he doesn't exchange his faithfulness for the father's love. For the father is always with him (you) and everything that belongs to the father is already his (yours). The radical grace—unearned, unmerited—is given to both sons not dependent on any prerequisites, work, or particular attitudes. This grace is really the great gift of an eccentric parent!

Who is truly prodigal, if not this parent? He is recklessly extravagant and lavish with his love. His actions don't make sense in an eBay world because our culture has shaped us to be suspicious of anything we do not earn or want to purchase. Grace doesn't make sense because we would rather have something we can pay for and therefore be good consumers who deserve it because we've paid for the products and services we've acquired.

Jesus ends his parable leaving us unsure how the two sons react to the prodigal father's grace. Did the younger son change and become more dutiful and responsible? Or did he run off again with some money bilked from his father (again!) to play the tables in Las Vegas? And the older brother: Did he come into the party sharing in the joy of the father? Or did he stand outside of the party resentfully objecting over and over at the unfairness of it all? Jesus appears to leave that question open to us. The question of repentance is important only in that it follows grace and does not precede it. The sons received the gift, and we are not quite sure what they do with it. The story, ultimately, is about the gift of the father, a gift as much to all those who hear the story as to the characters in the story. The story is about the eccentricity of grace.

THE ECCENTRICITY OF GRACE

The eccentricity of grace is prevalent through Jesus' life and teachings as the core way in which God relates to God's creation. Jesus was always reaching out to, praying for, healing, and eating with people considered undeserving of God's love, and his parables are filled with the countercultural nature of grace. Think about it: An owner of a vineyard pays the same amount to laborers who work for an hour as those who work for eight hours (Matt. 20:1–16). A shepherd abandons ninety-nine sheep to find the lost one (Luke 15:3–7)! A party is thrown celebrating God's powerful love and people are invited off the street (Matt. 22:1–10 and Luke 14:16–24)! One cannot read the Gospels without being struck by the prevailing, uncomfortable, and strange nature of grace that Jesus embodied and preached.

What is this grace? It is many things, in many varied forms, but at the heart it is God's great gift, not earned, but given out of God's abundance.

God's grace is the gift of continual forgiveness every day. Presbyterian chaplain and pastoral counselor, Dr. Steven Spidell, among others, has suggested that grace is God's judgment and God's mercy together intertwined; they are the dual elements of God's greatest gift. Grace creates the gift of salvation (wholeness), the gift of God's very presence in Jesus Christ— Emmanuel (God with us). Grace is being accepted fully and wholly, being welcomed and invited to share in the joy of creation. Grace is love freely shared without strings attached. It is all these things and, in some ways, none of them. Grace is the mystery of God who loves beyond logic and imagining! Maybe for that reason Jesus doesn't try to explain grace with a particular definition. He simply points, rather, to the truth and reality of grace by his actions and stories, and even his death.

Two noteworthy aspects of grace arise when we live in a world that places a particular value on persons, relationships, and institutions. First, grace is a way of seeing the entire world as a gift rather than a commodity, and all aspects of creation and life are, therefore, "grace-based." Our very existence is a gift given freely, to be cherished, nurtured, and enjoyed. The universe in all its diversity and beauty is a gift to be explored and appreciated. Faith itself is not something earned by dint of our will or actions, but comes, unbidden, often in the darkest times in our life when we are afraid and filled with doubts. The grace-based gift of God's relationship with God's people comes freely and challenges this worldview that (1) we earn what we get, and (2) therefore, we have a claim on the "stuff" of this world as commodities to be used for our particular benefit. In an eBay world where everything has a price, grace makes everything truly priceless!

The second aspect of grace that counters our eBay world is grace's way of transforming persons into human beings rather than consumers or commodities. The story of the prodigal father is about seeing human beings for what they are and not for what they can pay in repentance or guilt. The father embraces both sons because they are his sons and not because of what they do for him. The illogic of grace is the view of the other not as a commodity that meets our needs, but as one whose gifts are to be cherished in and of themselves. The radical nature of grace is that seeing the other as God's gift even extends to people we may consider enemies.

One can see the eccentricity of this grace in an eBay world. The giftedness of God's love, unmerited and unearned, runs counter to the very way our cultures envision life. Grace (1) challenges the hyperconsumerism, which understands that everything has a price, and (2) calls into question hypercapitalism, which sees everything and everyone in service to the consumer.

The very eccentricity of God's grace makes it difficult to comprehend and raises difficult questions for us to answer. Does the idea that God freely gives salvation make it cheap? If grace calls us to live not for self-satisfaction and consumption but for the other, could that not also cheapen our relationships with other people if they do not deserve our love?

IS GRACE CHEAP?

Dietrich Bonhoeffer (whom we learn more about later) once wrote a book called *The Cost of Discipleship*.[4] In this book he challenged Christians not to embrace "cheap" grace nor to be under any illusions that such a thing as easy Christianity exists. In his discussion of cheap grace, Bonhoeffer uses the market as a metaphor. "Cheap grace means grace sold on the market like cheapjake wares. The sacraments, the forgiveness of sin, and the consolations of religion are thrown away at cut prices."[5] On the one hand, Bonhoeffer is critical of grace as another commodity. Yet his use of the language of cheap and costly can easily create confusion about the nature of grace. We do not think Bonhoeffer intended this interpretation. We believe a better word expresses Bonhoeffer's intention than "costly" grace, which implies something to be bought. Instead we could call grace "priceless." Grace is so precious that it cannot be bought or sold on the spiritual market.

Grace is not cheap because it is priceless. Grace is priceless because God gave something freely that could not be bought. This gift was God in Jesus Christ, who "did not regard equality with God as something to be exploited, but emptied himself taking the form of a slave, . . . humbled himself and became obedient to the point of death—even death on a cross."[6] Bonhoeffer is not arguing that grace is simply one commodity (Jesus) traded for another (our sin). Instead the very pricelessness is that God came to God's world for God's people simply out of the abundance of God's mercy and not because we exchange good deeds for it. God's love is priceless because it is grace.

"When Christ calls a man, he calls him to die."[7] Discipleship, for Bonhoeffer, does not precede grace, but results from it. When grace takes hold of us, grace calls us out from selfishness and self-centeredness into the world. In fact, grace is the call. Grace, with its dual components of God's judgment and God's mercy, transforms and changes us so that we may serve Christ in the world. Cheap grace is the belief that forgiveness of sins is an end in itself; therefore, I can simply come to church on Sunday morning and hear my sins are forgiven and go out feeling justified, yet without genuinely being any different from the world around me.

Priceless grace calls into question the very idea in our world that faith is about being justified unto ourselves. If faith were only a personal feeling of self-justification, then grace would be (and is) cheapened. Remember, grace is priceless in the very fact that it transforms us, causes the self to die and follow Jesus—not simply to morning worship or Wednesday evening choir practice, but into the world. Grace costs us all self-centeredness and selfishness because it changes us and, in fact, destroys the very selves we labor so desperately to hold on to.

In truth, grace sets us free to serve the Lord of heaven and earth not out of a sense of paying what is due or because others are in our debt. Grace gives us the freedom to love ourselves for the giftedness of life and to love others for who they are in the giftedness of creation. Grace is really "the gift that keeps on giving."

Alex tells the story of his son's birth. He met his wife, Teresa, when they both were a little older, and when they married they decided to start their family sooner than later. To their surprise and chagrin, Teresa became pregnant on their honeymoon. After the initial shock, they grew excited about the upcoming birth, especially when they went in for their first sonogram. Alex was beside himself when they found the baby was going to be a boy, and hardly noticed the sonogram technician looking a little worried as she explored the whole baby. The technician said that she could not find the stomach, but not to be alarmed because often a baby doesn't swallow amniotic fluid and therefore the stomach doesn't appear on the screen. She told them to come back in a week or two, and she would be able to find the stomach. Teresa and Alex excitedly showed off the sonogram pictures of their new son, Noah, without giving the problem a second thought.

When they returned a week later, the sonogram technician became more and more somber as she searched for the stomach and began to take notes. Alex and Teresa became particularly anxious as they were called into the doctor's office. He said he may have bad news. Possibly the baby still just was not swallowing amniotic fluid at this time, but the problem could be far more serious. A blockage could be preventing the amniotic fluid from reaching the stomach. There were other ominous signs, too: the baby looked to have a rather large head with short legs and, with the possible blockage, that may indicate the child has Down's syndrome. The doctor was sending them to a specialist to see what he could find. The appointment was scheduled for a week later.

That week was one of the hardest of their lives as they struggled with the possibility of their child being mentally disabled and physically challenged. The week was full of anxiety and fear as they tried to comprehend what their life would be like with a Down's syndrome child, but during that difficult week Alex and Teresa realized something. While they certainly hoped things would turn out well, what they came to understand was that the results of the sonogram really didn't matter. No matter how the child turned out, no matter what he looked like, no matter how little his intelligence may be, Alex and Teresa would love him for who he was.

The week passed and the two of them went to the specialist, who hooked up the sonogram and, lo and behold, right there was the stomach. Noah just hadn't swallowed any fluid and thus was simply being as contrary as his dad. When Alex asked about the big head and short legs, the doctor simply looked him up and down and said, "Like father, like son!"

While that week had been difficult and scary, Alex caught a glimpse of grace. He began to catch a glimmer of how God loves us, not because we might be attractive, intelligent, or athletically gifted. God loves us because we are God's children no matter what. God's love is not dependent on any particular thing we do or accomplish. God's love comes to us as a gift out of the infinite love of a parent for a child, and this radical gift shapes and transforms our lives. In an eBay world, that gift may seem irrational and illogical. But thank God, it is a gift.

NOTES AND JOURNALING OPPORTUNITIES

I.   Parts of this chapter with which I have mostly agreed in the past:

II. Parts of this chapter with which I have mostly disagreed in the past:

III. Parts of this chapter which have presented new thoughts or information for me:

IV. What's in this chapter . . .

(a) prompts me to remember

(b) prompts me, from years past, to wonder about

(c) prompts me to want to ask, to investigate, to research

(d) prompts me to wonder about changing

(e) prompts me to wonder about the near future in the following ways

(f) prompts me to wonder about the more distant future in the following ways

V. Personal writings, sketches, drawings related to this chapter

Can We Hang with the Names on Jesus' Buddy List?

Humility in an In-Your-Face World

"It's Hard to Be Humble"
—title of a Mac Davis song[1]

A N IMPORTANT NOTE: In this and the next three chapters we explore various understandings and experiences of faith that play a key role in the lives of Jesus' disciples across the centuries, including our lives during the early twenty-first century.

While we are not the first, and will not be the last, to think or write about some of the topics and related issues of the next few chapters, some of this material (or our angles of approach) may be new to you. Feel free to disagree. Also, please become engaged with us in an exploration of areas ripe for potential growth of faith, discipleship, and mutuality among God's people.

Additionally, let us be clear about what is most basic: Neither this chapter nor the chapters following attempt to debate the existence of God. For us, as the two coauthors, God's existence is a given. Neither do these chapters debate the lordship of Jesus Christ. For us, that also is a given. We, nevertheless, cite examples of ways disciples of Jesus across the years and around the globe have held, and continue to hold, a variety of opinions and convictions. Such approaches and ways of "living out discipleship" have varied, therefore, in method and perspective. We believe we can grow through what we observe and learn from studying others' lives as much as by examining, in God's grace, our own.

In her novel, *Cold Sassy Tree,* set in small-town Georgia in 1937, author Olive Burns tells of Grandpa's marriage after Grandma died. This development is problematic for many townspeople, extended family, and church members even though it is fine with Grandpa. Many judge that he is not observing a long enough and respectful enough period of mourning. Consequently, at the local Presbyterian church, Grandpa no longer feels welcome. He feels harshly judged. He feels his bride is not received respectfully. Therefore, they stay at home on Sunday morning. Not to deny themselves the sacrament of the Lord's Supper, though, Grandpa takes out cake and cola. He slices, pours, and celebrates, even though his new spouse is not quite certain their celebration is legitimate. Grandpa's confidence may seem arrogant and blasphemous to some traditional Presbyterians and other church folk. They may be offended. Other persons who've felt cold-shouldered or excluded, conversely, may understand Grandpa's boldness in faith with sympathy, great appreciation, and some sense of humor.[2] For the next several pages, we consider how persons can be disciples of Jesus with both boldness and humility, while relating to other persons with grace-based respect.

BUDDY LISTS

People who have computers and Internet access know that their electronic address books provide easy access to the names of those to whom one frequently writes. In addition to address books, buddy lists allow quick access to instant message conversations, which are kind of like half telephone conversation and half Morse code.

The names on our buddy lists are usually just that: friends or acquaintances with whom we have much in common. Buddies not only instant message one another, they also hang with one another, spending time together.

Jesus' buddy list included a wider variety of people than traditionally religious persons ever wanted to "hang with"! Jesus' buddy list included small children; government treasury agents; corner merchants; farmers; laborers; prostitutes; persons with fevers, epilepsy, leprosy, arthritis, schizophrenia, multiple personalities, and hemorrhages (bleeding); non-Americans; non-Jews; non-Christians; "high-up" religious leaders; street-corner panhandlers; Roman soldiers; and others. Is that list varied enough?

We might ask ourselves: Is my buddy list that varied? Granted, you're not Jesus, and neither are we. The buddy list of your church or Bible study group also may not be as varied as Jesus' buddy list in his day and time.

In a world where electronic and satellite communications "shrink everything," the neighbor around the globe and the neighbor across town are those with whom we know we are connected and related as God's family, as much as we together are part of the world community. How can we be prepared for the complex relationships into which God calls us, both with those already on our buddy lists and with those who might be on Jesus' buddy list but whom we'd prefer not to have on ours?

As we noted in chapter 3, God's "great gift" (g.g.) is grace. For those who would be disciples of Jesus, in a postmodern ethos and dot.com world as much as in any other setting, the four "essential indicators" (e.i.) are humility, gratitude, community, and courage. In this chapter we explore humility. The next three chapters consider the others.

HUMILITY

The first essential indicator of being a disciple of Jesus is *humility*. What is it? Humility is a developed characteristic and quality in one's life that believes and demonstrates in relationships that every person's foundation for personhood is grace and only grace (whether any person recognizes that fact and foundation or not). Humility is not the seedbed for relativism for believing there's no "real" right or wrong, only differences. Humility, for a disciple of Jesus, relies both on Jesus' teachings, which interpret the Jewish Scriptures, and on his life, which exemplifies those teachings and interpretations.

While we need not rewrite the apostle Paul's "classic" list of nine "fruit(s) of the Spirit" from Galatians 5:22–23 ("love, joy, peace, patience, kindness, generosity, faithfulness, gentleness, and self-control"), looking for additional descriptions may be helpful. The letter known as Ephesians also includes (4:1–2) a description of disciples of Jesus: "I therefore, the prisoner in the Lord, beg you to lead a life worthy of the calling to which you have been called, with all humility and gentleness, with patience, bearing with one another in love, making every effort to maintain the unity of the Spirit in the bond of peace."

Ephesians was written to a community (or group of communities) in which the citizens were aware of many differences existing among themselves locally and in other regions throughout the Roman Empire, differences that were religious, ethnic, economic, and cultural. Given such differences and (one can easily imagine) given multiple differences of opinions, to create humility takes grace. When humility is an active ingredient, Jesus' disciples live with respect relating to one another and to others.

Any diagnosis probing a lack of respect and humility between human beings will be incomplete if the investigation fails to go at least as deep as the identity of every individual. Remember, according to Genesis 1:27, every individual (*every* individual!) is created "in the image of God."

Beyond being created in God's image, Paul asserts in 1 Corinthians 15:49, "Just as we have borne the image of the man of dust, we will also bear the image of the man of heaven." In other words, as much as we are created in God's image, by God's redeeming love, through life and beyond death, we are also being transformed in the image of Jesus! Each one of us has hope of growing in the Lord! In the words of the psalmist and the revival worshiper: "Hallelujah!"

If my religious belief is perfect, or even superior, can I be genuinely humble? Humility (the first e.i.) does not come easily, even though God's grace—freely given—is the source gift. (Be careful to whom you say, "Humility does not come easily." A person might respond to you as someone did to us: "Foote and Thornburg, why doesn't humility come easily to y'all? You two have so much to be humble about!")

Humility does not come easily, though, because humility has so much to overcome. Or, rather, God's grace has so much to overcome in order for genuine humility to gain even a toehold in our lives and the lives of all of God's people!

(It would be easy to write an entire book on how much humility has to overcome to play a role in the lives of human beings. We'll try to do it here with a few pages. Maybe you can write that entire book.)

During the last few decades of the twentieth century, Mac Davis sang about a difficulty some of God's people face on a regular basis: genuinely confessing "it's hard to be humble." This action is tough, confesses the singer (we presume, tongue in cheek), anytime one thinks of oneself as "perfect in every way."[3]

Writing in Romans 3:23, the apostle Paul reminds us that "all (people) have sinned and fall short of the glory of God." In other words, no one is perfect. Almost all, if not all, disciples of Jesus agree with Paul's saying that we all sin. Immediately, though, a crack, a fissure, a crevice, or a canyon begins to divide certain disciples of Jesus from certain others.

Although most of Jesus' disciples agree that no one is "perfect in every way," many, if not all, disciples of Jesus have believed at some point in life that "the Christian way" or "a certain Christian way" of believing is a perfect or at least a superior way to believe. The statement that Christianity provides a "perfect (or superior) belief" is worth exploring. (Hang on now! Furrowed brows and stomachs oozing acidic secretions are common in this "territory.")

Some disciples of Jesus prefer to believe Christianity provides a perfect (or superior) belief because they (and we) have been taught by grandparents, parents, church, or culture that "this is so." Here we meet the influence of premodernism. According to the premodern perspective, a statement is accurate or true because someone has taught it as being accurate or true. You or I, we or they, become convinced that the teaching is credible. We are willing to accept a given teaching as authoritative because we accept the teacher or the experience one has experienced as having authority for one's life.

As an example of a premodern way of thinking, the church and the culture taught for centuries that the earth was the center of the solar system "because they said so," from both their own interpretation of Scripture and their own interpretation of personal observation and experience in the world. Scientists Copernicus, Kepler, and Galileo faced an uphill challenge (and possible accusations of heresy) when they, following their research, included among their professional arguments the suggestion that the sun, rather than the earth, was the center of the solar system.[4] Their method was the method of modernism, at a time when the ethos was predominantly premodern. Church and culture were resistant to these suggestions (and not humble about it). They (church and culture) were convinced that they were perfect in every way, or, if not perfect, perfect enough to pass judgment harshly on others.

Religious belief, though, can result from sources and avenues beyond the premodern. Many people would say that belief among Jesus' disciples across the centuries sprouts from the soil of Scripture. They (and we, the coauthors) believe the collection of writings called Scripture communicates the story and word of God among God's people through the centuries. Many persons further believe that religious belief and doctrine can be argued logically and persuasively from the teachings of Scripture, the findings of archaeology, and other sources and methods. (The two of us as coauthors tend not to believe as much as some others that belief and doctrine can be argued and "proved" logically.) To the extent that such convictions are part of someone's belief system, we can classify such believers as theologians and thinkers operating under the umbrella of modernism.

One may be convinced that religious faith is true because "the tradition" or a trusted person says it's true (premodern). One may also be convinced that religious faith is true because Scripture, archaeology, logic, etc., make a compelling case for the religion being true (modernism).

In either case, humility is important. In neither case does humility automatically result. For two reasons, humility and religious conviction do not easily go hand in hand. First, we disciples of Jesus have a tendency to begin interpreting Scripture in ways that oversimplify. We frequently (almost with a reflex action) think and categorize with "opposites," such as "saved" and "unsaved," "church" and "world," "pure" and "impure," "evil" and "good." Jesus' Great Commission is one example:

> All authority in heaven and on earth has been given to me. Go therefore and make disciples of all nations, baptizing them in the name of the Father and of the Son and of the Holy Spirit, and teaching them to obey everything that I have commanded you. And remember, I am with you always, to the end of the age. (Matt. 28:18b–20)

Disciples of Jesus have all too frequently heard words like "authority," "commanded," "teachings," and "obey," along with the imperative voice of "go" and "make," and felt licensed by Jesus to pressure and coerce others, even against those others' hesitations and reluctance. (How ironic that Christians criticize other religious traditions for practices that seem coercive: for example, stories told of the ninth- and tenth-century spread of Islam "by the point of the sword.")

Another, quite possibly more helpful, way to "hear" and interpret Matthew 28:18b–20 understands Jesus as a rabbi (religious teacher) instructing disciples in ways to develop a community of faithful followers. That instruction can be done with humility and with boldness, yet without pressure and coercion (more about "boldness" in later paragraphs). In fact, Jesus does this without rejecting or even scolding disciples who "doubted" as they worshiped (Matt. 28:17). What does that tell us about the need to be respectful of one another, particularly toward those whose faith seems severely challenged, even ailing? If Jesus preferred moving on with the commissioning rather than being bigheaded and putting down the doubters because of any feeling of superiority, how important for the rest of us to give that style a try!

Additionally, so much of Jesus' teachings in Matthew are words directed to religious leaders who are focused almost completely on ensuring the fulfillment of religious rules and practices, while keeping a safe distance from all others not in "compliance." (We explore this issue of who's closer to God's holiness, and who is not, in chapter 8.) As Jesus views the situation, such religious leaders, plus all who imitate their teachings and practices, reveal a lack of humility, a lack of compassion, and an inability to see all other persons as God's gifts.

People can read Matthew's chapters and conclude that Jesus was talking only to Jewish religious leaders. Another (and, we believe, more helpful) way to hear and interpret Jesus' teachings is to understand that they are intended to promote, in any period of time and in any place, humility, compassion, and respect for every human being. Those teachings are for all who would be God's faithful people, both for religious leaders two thousand years ago and for every one of us today!

Following this interpretation, humility is more than an element of character. It also can be considered as "a way of relating." If you want to test your "humility quotient" (or anyone else's humility quotient), then ask if you (or they) can gladly sing the following ditty (sung to the tune of "If You're Happy and You Know It"):

> When your attitude is prideful, you can fall.
> When your attitude is prideful, you can fall.
> When your attitude is prideful, You may hope you're best of all.
> When your attitude is prideful, you can fall.

> If you can't discern you're veering, you'll get stuck.
> If you can't discern you're veering, you'll get stuck.
> If you can't discern you're veering, You will end up in the muck.
> If you can't discern you're veering, you'll get stuck.

> If you're faking being human, it's so sad.
> If you're faking being human, it's so sad.
> If you're faking being human, Then the Lord cannot be glad.
> If you're faking being human, it's so sad.

> As God's grace enfolds the world, we are well.
> As God's grace enfolds the world, we are well.
> As God's grace enfolds the world, We are healed beyond what's hell.
> As God's grace enfolds the world, we are well.

Confidence for life in faith, then, is related to trust in God's grace. Confidence for life in faith is never healthily related to certainty that my faith or discipleship efforts are superior or more perfect than yours or someone else's.

Second, continually standing in the way of genuine humility's growth and development is triumphalism. What is triumphalism? It's a developed characteristic and quality in one's life which believes and demonstrates in relationships that a particular belief, priority, or allegiance that one adopts is superior to all others' respective beliefs, priorities, or allegiances.

In short, triumphalism asserts that "My preference will beat your preference, so you'd be smart to come over to 'my side.'" Or, put another way,

"We're number one!" What's beneath or behind triumphalism? At the root of or behind the stage of much of our triumphalism is fear, fear of existing while being regarded as second-class or fifth-class, fear of being subjected to an overlord or an overclass, or fear of being a person without full worth, esteem, and dignity.

People have reason to feel that way. In the words of the apostle Paul (Rom. 8:38–39, KJV and RSV), "principalities" and "powers" have the capacity to create feelings and perceptions in us that we, as human beings, are either (1) less in value than someone else, or (2) separated from God's love and power. "Principalities" can describe overbearing, authoritarian individuals or overbearing, authoritarian groups. They can be religious or secular in nature, or national, ethnic, or sectarian in nature. "Powers" can be addictions, compulsions, tyrannies, fears, passions, or apathy. They can be individualized, corporate or cultural, attitudinal or relational.

When one feels oppressed or inferior, a reaction of defensiveness can result. Protesting against such feelings, one might justifiably exclaim, "Yes, I am worth something!" That reaction can be a positive (holy) natural response. Put another way, "God doesn't make junk! God only makes high quality!"

Such sensitivity to feeling oppressed or inferior, however, can lead to triumphalism. The value that God gives may not be perceived or believed. A person may not be convinced that the high value and regard in which God holds that person is adequate to "fill the bill" at a certain time in one's life. A person who deep down feels oppressed or inferior often seeks to compensate by asserting himself or herself against others, often in unhealthy ways.

Triumphalism wants to "win." Triumphalism wants to win with a smile, being nice, or to win with a snarl, being aggressive. The style doesn't matter. What's important is having others either "join up" or "bow down" to recognize that I am (or my group is) justified enough and strong enough to have my (or its) will be the will that prevails.

Disciples of Jesus have long debated the interpretation of Scripture verses similar to one of Jesus' "I am" sayings in the Gospel according to John (14:6): "I am the way, and the truth, and the life. No one comes to the Father except through me."

People who teach from such passages frequently want to bleach the mystery and the humility from faith and community. They forget or ignore that in the same Gospel account (John), Jesus speaks of having "other sheep" (10:16) and of there being "many dwelling places" in my "Father's house" (14:2).

When reading Scripture today, we encounter layers and layers of experience, custom, and tradition that influence and condition our hearing and

interpretation. If reading Scripture uncritically (without careful consideration of those layers and layers), we draw conclusions based upon the
interpretations of many others, and we assume Jesus intended to teach
exactly as later interpreters tell us that he intended to teach.

One traditionally accepted (or ignored!) teaching from Scripture is
Matthew 5:48, with Jesus' exhortation for disciples to "[b]e perfect, therefore, as your heavenly Father is perfect." The word translated to English
as "perfect" does not mean "flawless, pure, and uncontaminated by
human influence." The Greek word, rather, has a definition more like
"being made whole," "being made complete," or "living toward the
ultimate goal." When Jesus is quoted here, the teaching may be more along
the lines of "Live toward God's ultimate goal, transformed for loving even
enemies." That approach differs significantly from simply, "Be perfect and
flawless, as you want the sound that your stereo produces to be perfect
and flawless!"

Do You Mean We're Not Number One?

The early Christian communities (with their several similarities and differences) struggled for survival. Claiming Jesus to be God's promised deliverer,
theirs was a minority proposition (with varied interpretations and
emphases according to which teacher a person followed most closely).
Christians (disciples of Jesus) were fewer in number than the other religious, cultural, commercial, and political groups within the Roman
Empire. Other established religious groups did not want competition (naturally) from any new group (or groups) that would compete for citizens' or
members' loyalty. The minority Christian communities needed to be
emboldened in the face of cultural majorities seeking to keep competing
groups "in check" or seeking to eliminate the competition. The letters to
Christian faith communities and the Gospel accounts served this embold-
ening purpose, as well as articulating differences between Christian leaders
themselves.[5]

Obviously, a huge problem develops for humility when any of three
types of fears begins to be stirred in one's life and one's community: (1) fear
of not being "number one" any longer; (2) fear of "losing" one's position,
even if already less than number one; and (3) fear of being eliminated.

When a person or group fears losing one's position and no longer being
"number one," majoritarianism can turn ugly. When a person or group
fears losing one's position lower than "number one," or fears being eliminated, minoritarianism can turn ugly. (Remember how various groups have

inflicted "ethnic cleansings" and unimaginable violence upon others, even in the twentieth century and into the twenty-first?)

The problems related to majoritarianism and minoritarianism have plagued Christianity over and over since Emperor Constantine the Great declared Christianity to be the sanctioned religion of the Empire (in 323). Christianity went from minority status to majority status almost overnight. The Scriptures that had been giving encouragement to a minoritarian group did not change. Those Scriptures were the same, yet the life situation of the commuities with disciples of Jesus as members changed immensely. Soon disciples of Jesus were reading what we know as the New Testament from a majoritarian perspective, when so much of it (if not all of it) was intended for a community with minoritarian status.

Triumphalism and aggressive attitudes (either offensive or defensive) are not limited to groups in the majority who could be labeled as "conservatives" or "liberals," "traditionalists," "progressives," or "revolutionaries." In a great spoof on people who call themselves "liberal," Peter DeVries wrote of a character, the Reverend Andrew Mackerel, who was pastor of Peoples' Liberal Congregation. DeVries tells that the Reverend Mackerel called the city zoning commission's office to protest when an attention-grabbing green and orange "Jesus Saves" billboard was raised within view of his office window. He complained to the office clerk that the sign was offensive: "How do you expect me to write a sermon with that thing staring me in the face?"

Suppose "liberals" in the Reverend Mackerel's community constitute a minority of the population. Novelist DeVries pokes fun at how a member or leader of a minority group can compete, seek to triumph, and be as aggressive as many members of a majority group.[6]

While the Reverend Mackerel's protest is in no way a persecution against others, we could develop a pages-long list from century to century naming majority and minority groups both persecuting others in order to advance their respective causes. As often as individuals and groups coerce or persecute others for political reasons, individuals and groups coerce and persecute others in the name of religion. To make such an observation or discovery is sad, but people who have coerced and persecuted others while professing their own religious faith as Christian usually are personally convinced that what they are doing reflects the will of Jesus, the Prince of Peace.

Can I Be Evangelical and Humble?

If Jesus is our example, God obviously prefers a humility that is healthily confident and respectfully bold. Disciples of Jesus through the centuries have been encouraged to be evangelical: to be those who share the story and teachings of God's good news of grace (God's judgment and mercy!) in Jesus, the Christ.

This statement raises the question: Can one be an evangelical disciple of Jesus without being triumphalistic? We think so, especially if one can sing with honesty and joy the ditty printed on page 47. If one cannot sing (or pray) those simple verses, then one's "humility quotient" may be dangerously low.

The biblical story is certainly life changing—before, during, and after Jesus' birth, life, ministry, death, and resurrection because God has mysterious and wondrous ways of creating, calling, redeeming, and transforming God's people over the short term and over the longer term. The story of God with God's people is worth exploring with others in relationships of mutuality. This story is worth studying and considering with others, many of whom have not or do not experience life in the same way as you or someone else who is a disciple of Jesus.

Yes, one can be evangelical and not triumphalistic, but not without reviewing and evaluating (1) one's own attitudes, words, and actions and (2) the story of faith communities that have said they live by faith in the Lord. The second of these two is as critical as the first. Groups in general, and religious groups as much as any other, conveniently and quickly develop amnesia about dark episodes and unfortunate behavior by individuals and groups who are members of their particular tradition (or "family").

Like a dysfunctional family, we humans resist therapeutically seeking the facts of the past. This resistance to discover past facts and apply their relevance to our present and future reduces our potential for living healthily as God's people now and in the time to come. Many (or most) church leaders unfortunately resist the efforts of women and men and girls and boys to discover the sad chapters or thorny issues in our faith traditions' histories. (Some of that resistance can be termed "institutional." Institutional leaders resist because if "family secrets" are out in the open, the credibility of the institution may be called into question.)

We can learn so much from such studies, though. Some people might say that a group (an "institution") without "open records" and the encouragement of wide-ranging dialogue is not worth believing, joining, or continuing with membership unless as much of the whole truth as can be discovered is known. When that degree of honesty exists, we are able to relate to others based on God's grace as the "great gift" (g.g.), with humility as the first essential indicator (e.i.).

If one is to be evangelical and not triumphalistic, one must develop relationships that are not based on another person's potential "worth" as a convert to Christianity. Relationships between persons are most healthily based on the other person being a child of God, a brother or sister in God's family. That's all. Respectful relationships are not based on one person's (my) need for another person to "get to the same point of view" or the same experience and understanding of faith that is meaningful to the first person (me).

The "Duck Test"

One can usually evaluate one's own (or any person's) thoughts, words, and actions with respect to triumphalism by adapting the well-known "duck test": "If it looks like a duck, walks like a duck, flies like a duck, swims like a duck, sounds like a duck, and smells like a duck, it probably is a duck." If it looks like triumphalism, etc., it probably is triumphalism. Being evangelical without being triumphalistic is possible. It's not possible, though, without continual self-examination in the light of the ministry and spirit of Jesus.

Earlier in the chapter we noted that "If Jesus is our example, God obviously prefers a humility that is healthily confident and respectfully bold." If one is attempting to develop humility in one's attitude and relationships, how do healthy confidence and respectful boldness become part of the equation? We've already noted how we can healthily challenge institutional "defenders" who resist probing studies of history, relationships, and logic.

Exploring how to develop a healthy confidence and respectful boldness is important for two reasons: (1) much traditional Christian teaching is, unfortunately, based on "niceness" (misinterpreting Jesus' blessing upon "the meek"), with Christians being discouraged from saying anything in opposition to someone who is claiming more authority or credibility than can be justifiable; and (2) the "principalities and powers" continually attempt to intimidate and suppress healthy confidence and respectful boldness among God's people. The first of these statements may be based on not wanting to disturb, or muddy, the waters. The second may be based on principalities and powers wanting to bring God's good creations (persons!) to a level lower than the pitifully low (and thereby inflated) self-esteem of the principalities and powers themselves.

Both factors are unfortunate because the Scriptures tell of God's encouraging incredible boldness in the lives of Moses, Deborah, Elijah, Amos, Jeremiah, Esther, Jesus, and Paul, to name just a few.

Consider the following instant message conversation between two high school students:

Hoopster: how r u?

Drumlass: ok i guess. u?

Hoopster: about me in a minute. u just ok?

Drumlass: actually, really ticked. after band this a.m., while headed to eng class, sherry asked will if he'd like to meet her cousin comin to visit this weekend.

Hoopster: what'd he say?

Drumlass: he would if she wasn't as religious as sherry.

Hoopster: cold. sherry said?

Drumlass: on second thought, maybe her cousin would prefer to meet a brain without a body than a body without a brain.

Hoopster: verrrry cold. was will bleeding on the walkway?

Drumlass: hardly. he said he had a brain, and that's why he didn't want to go out with anyone too born again.

Hoopster: back to sherry?

Drumlass: she said, even if my cousin thought you were hot, I'd tell her a wrapped box might not have a gift inside.

Hoopster: whad he say?

Drumlass: that in his case the gift inside was as good as his looks on the outside.

Hoopster: and?

Drumlass: she said she must be mistaken cuz she'd seen more handsome driving down the road behind a trailer full of horses.

Hoopster: sounds like sherry needs no lessons in backtalk.

Drumlass: i guess not. will was so rude to start with.

Hoopster: people are rude. some start it. others give back cause it's deserved.

Drumlass: i guess, but my solution is washing everybody's mouth out with soap.

Hoopster: won't that just make suds?

Drumlass: suds and a memory not soon forgotten.

Hoopster: fine with me. got2go. dad says supper's ready. call later if you want, or I'll catch you tomorrow.

Drumlass: sounds good. bye.

Hoopster: c u lata

Send Save

Sharp words make a point and can have a healthy role to play.

Drumlass observed a portion of Will's thoughts and attitudes as she overheard the conversation Sherry had with him on the way between band and English. What he demonstrated of his thoughts and attitudes seemed rather arrogant, distancing, and "put-downish" toward Sherry and her cousin. Do you think Sherry's "comebacks" demonstrated a type of arrogance and that she should have said "Suit yourself" or "Your loss," and let it go at that? Or did her comebacks demonstrate a "healthy confidence and respectful boldness" that challenged Will in a positive way? Why or why not? How did Will's words indicate a certain defensiveness and desire to protect his space from a new or different relationship?

THE POTATO-FACE BLIND MAN'S "ZINGER"

In Carl Sandburg's stories known as *The Rootabaga Tales,* he describes the "potato face blind man," who, in fact, can actually "see" more of God's gifts in the world than many "sighted" people. One zinger in Sandburg's description of this character is the hand-printed sign that the potato-faced blind man has attached to his left sleeve: "I, too, am blind."[7]

Blind and Mortal!

The primary additional reason for a grace-based humility—with healthy confidence and respectful boldness—as an attitude and a foundation for relationships is the fact that we are all mortal. We all die. No dreams or attitudes or pretensions keep us from that common experience. We are born. We die. In between, God's word—through spirit, Scripture, and history—invites and calls us to grow in realizing how grace makes possible living a "more fully human life" as God intends. So, what does "living a more fully human life" look like?

In 1956, Mark Harris wrote a baseball-based novel titled *Bang the Drum Slowly,* which was made into a movie in 1973 featuring Robert DeNiro. It's the story of a "first-rate" major league pitcher named Henry Wiggin (played by Michael Moriarty) who befriends a "second-rate" catcher named Arthur (nicknamed "Bruce") Pearson. Bruce is dying of Hodgkin's lymphoma but no one except Henry, Henry's wife, Bruce, and Bruce's parents know that Bruce is dying. Henry wants to finish the season with Bruce still on the team. The story features several great lines as their team eventually becomes aware of Bruce's struggle. One of the greatest, though, is when Bruce is thinking about (1) other players "giving him a hard time" because he's not of All-Star quality as a catcher and (2) his illness. He says to Henry, "Probably everybody would be nice to you if they knew you were dying." Henry responds, "Everybody knows everybody is dying. . . . That is why people are nice. We all die soon enough, so why not be nice to each other?"[8]

We've previously noted how "being nice" as a virtue which never speaks up for justice or dignity is not what is meant biblically by humility. Henry Wiggin's comments, though, could be translated: "That is why people are appropriately humble. We all die soon enough, so why not treat one another as fully human?"

If disciples of Jesus in the twenty-first century continually understand and confess (1) our basic blindness together with all of God's people, and (2) our common mortality with all of God's people, then we'll be praying for, working on, and monitoring the development of a healthy confidence and a respectful boldness. We'll also be subject to the spirit of God transforming us for "hanging with" that infinite variety of persons who are part of Jesus' buddy list, whether they know they're on that buddy list or not, and whether we're initially comfortable with them or not.

NOTES AND JOURNALING OPPORTUNITIES

I.   Parts of this chapter with which I have mostly agreed in the past:

II. Parts of this chapter with which I have mostly disagreed in the past:

III. Parts of this chapter which have presented new thoughts or information for me:

IV. What's in this chapter . . .

   (a) prompts me to remember

   (b) prompts me, from years past, to wonder about

   (c) prompts me to want to ask, to investigate, to research

   (d) prompts me to wonder about changing

   (e) prompts me to wonder about the near future in the following ways

   (f) prompts me to wonder about the more distant future in the following ways

V. Personal writings, sketches, drawings related to this chapter

What Would Jesus Drive?[1]

Gratitude in an All-You-Can-Eat World

> *"I B VAIN"*
> —Personalized license plate
> on a new Mercedes-Benz

A man was driving alone through central Texas when he pulled into a gas station and asked for directions: "Can you tell me how to get to Brownwood, Texas, from here?"

The owner of the station pointed in the same westerly direction the man had been driving and replied, "Straight ahead, eighty-five miles."

Apparently not satisfied, the man pointed toward the north and asked, "But isn't there a shortcut if I turn here?"

The owner of the station said, "I don't know how long it would take you if you went in that direction. I do know you can go straight west in the direction you're headed, and it's eighty-five miles. You can also go back due east, but it's about twenty-five thousand miles further."

The driver, who seemed not to appreciate the station owner's final assessment, sped off in the westerly direction said to offer the shortest route.

In a postmodern ethos, exploring and evaluating various directions and possibilities is quite acceptable, and we may discover, at times, that the most helpful route is one different from straight ahead. Shortcuts may or may not exist; even with shortcuts, a person may find a more circuitous route valuable. In considering gratitude, this chapter suggests a more circuitous route.

Why a more circuitous route? Let's back up and take a "running start" at this: If grace is God's "great gift" (g.g.) and if humility is the first "essential indicator" (e.i.) of the presence of grace in the lives of Jesus' disciples, one might say that gratitude is the second e.i.

GRATITUDE

Gratitude, though, is never as simple as someone telling us, "You ought to be grateful because. . . ." Any number of simple "ought-type" reasons can be listed, and those reasons are usually very simple (oversimplified) cause-and-effect reasons. Moreover, such reasons are frequently based on comparisons of one person's life (yours) with someone else in a tougher life situation.

In the tradition of *Late Night* talk-show host, David Letterman (and with apologies to him), we offer the following:

Top-Ten Inadequate but Often-Said Reasons to Be Grateful

10. At least some of your clothes are "name brand" from recognized designers.
9. You don't live in the Sudan or North Korea, where people are starving.
8. Your food is bought inside the grocery store or restaurant, not salvaged from their trash bins out back.
7. Unlike your parent(s), you don't have to walk to school two miles in snow and home after school, because at least the school bus comes to your neighborhood.
6. If there are high prices due to a shortage, you can still afford to pay the going rate.
5. You've got cancer, but chemotherapy helps. (So don't complain even though you feel weaker than an earthworm in dirt dried from drought.)
4. You've got a job that pays more than someone doing the same work in Thailand.
3. You're better looking than someone somewhere.
2. You're smarter than someone somewhere.
1. Because I said you ought to be grateful.

Can you see how gratitude is never as simple as someone telling us, "You ought to be grateful because . . ."? Simple, or oversimplified, "ought-type" reasons can be invoked, yet those reasons either soon or eventually lose their punch. Such thinking is rarely compelling for much longer than it takes most of us to set aside brussels sprouts and reach for a bowl of vanilla ice cream on a fudge brownie. Consider the following explanations of why "ought-type" reasons for gratitude don't work:

1. Reasons for gratitude based on a rationale that "you ought to" because "I said so" are not compelling once some distance develops between oneself and the authoritarian person demanding one's gratitude.
2. Reasons for gratitude based on a rationale that "you ought to" because "the Bible says so" are not compelling either, if distance develops between oneself and one's accepted belief in a book (or books) of the Bible that teach giving to God or to a religious community in a certain way.
3. Reasons for gratitude based on a rationale that "you ought to" because "your situation could be worse, like someone else's situation surely is" simply are not compelling as soon as one is able to slip into an "out of sight, out of mind" strategy. If I don't think about them, what worry will I have for them?

Demanding or requiring that a person or persons be grateful and express gratitude doesn't last. Someone might be grateful for an hour or a day, a week or a month, or longer. Even so, gratitude—as an essential indicator of God's great gift of grace—is most lasting and evident in a person's life when that person has a long-term interweaving and blend of personal experience, understanding, and practice.

How might a circuitous route be more effective in exploring and enhancing for "the long haul" each person's experience, understanding, and practice of gratitude?

In the 1950s and 1960s, pinball machines in fast-food and recreation centers were as popular as video game machines were in the 1980s and 1990s. Let's imagine a pinball machine game named "Immensa Gratia" ("immense thanks" in Latin). Granted, that's not "Master Blaster," "Galactic Voyager," or "Combat across the Cosmos," in each of which one may accumulate points by obliterating one's enemies. For our purposes, a different model is probably desirable, especially since Jesus taught disciples the radical act of praying for those considered to be one's enemies.

In chapter 3, we noted that much activity in today's Western world is consumer- and acquisition-driven. If we are attempting to seek and adopt some models for our lives that differ from what's consumer- and acquisition-driven, let's pretend that Immensa Gratia does not ring up numerical points for final standings. Rather, this game notes (by way of a displayed circle or bar graph), the percentage of gratitude and thanks growing in a person's life when in contact with any of the following six pinball posts standing for life influences. Conversely, the percentage of gratitude and thanks one feels retreats when not making contact with these posts or influences in life:

Immensa Gratia Pinball Posts

1. God's Grace-Based Relationships with People
2. Not Because I Have To
3. Not Because I'm More Fortunate Than Others
4. I Can't Outgive God
5. Everything Is Stewardship
6. Joyful Gratitude Possible When Much Is Very Negative

Post 1. "God's grace-based relationships with people." Your Gratiagraph grows when the pinball hits this post, and you realize that gratitude originates and flows from a grace-based relationship that God establishes, initiates, and fulfills. In more contemporary lingo, God designs and engineers the existence and workings of grace (holy judgment and mercy—both!). Prior to one's pinball hitting post 1, we likely associate gratitude with a feeling someone tells you that you "ought" to feel (post 2, below) or with the good fortune of "not being as 'bad off' as certain others" (post 3, below). Given the way the Bible tells the story of God relating to God's people, the writers are as clear as humanly possible in asserting that God has the first word in the creation of the cosmos (Gen. 1:1) and that God will have the last word in the conclusion of the cosmos (Rev. 22:20–21).

Over and over in the Bible and in history, God's word and spirit call God's people to reevaluate matters in life because the past and present over and over "do not measure up" to God's intentions. We recognize biblical examples of this call to reevaluate life from (a) the story of the garden of Eden (Gen. 2, 3, and 4—more on this later); (b) the guidance offered by the Ten Commandments (Exod. 20 and Deut. 5) and related teachings (the Torah) of the Hebrew Scriptures (Old Testament); (c) the exhortations and corrections of Israel's faithful prophets (also from the Hebrew Scriptures/Old Testament); (d) Jesus' birth, ministry, death, and resurrection; and (e) the writings distributed among the congregations of the early (first-century) church ("d" and "e" being parts of the New Testament).

Additionally, we recognize examples of God's call to reevaluate life from the living examples of God's people and from the spoken and written words (historical and "fictional") of God's people, people we've known in our own lifetimes as well as those we've never known personally.

Post 2. "Not Because I Have To." Your Gratia-graph grows when the pinball hits this post, and you realize that gratitude is the desire to express thanks and appreciation that you genuinely sense because you feel grateful about positive developments have occurred, related to both God and God's people (not to you alone; not to you and God excluding others; not to you and others excluding God).

In the Gospel according to Luke (19:1–10), a personal encounter is described in which Jesus meets a tax collector named Zacchaeus. Though the crowd following Jesus grumbles when he is respectful of Zacchaeus, Jesus indicates that unswerving respect is the only appropriate way for human beings to relate to one another. Further, Zacchaeus's life is turned around by meeting and becoming acquainted with Jesus. Zacchaeus's response to his life being turned around is gratitude to God expressed in restoring moneys to people he had cheated, and restoring the moneys in excess of that which religious teachings required (the amount plus 20 percent penalty, according to Lev. 5:16 and Num. 5:7). Zacchaeus will repay the overcharged amounts by twenty times more than required!

Post 3. "Not Because I'm More Fortunate Than Others." Your Gratia-graph grows when the pinball hits this post because you have realized that being more fortunate than someone else is a problematic basis for gratitude. You may remember the parable Jesus told (Luke 18:9–14) about the Pharisee (a religious officer very devoted to consistent fulfillment of religious teachings in the traditions of Moses and the faithful prophets of Israel) and the publican (a tax collector—like Zacchaeus—under contract to the Roman authorities, often associated with "being on the take" in terms of overcharges, etc.).

The Pharisee's prayer began, "God, I thank you that I am not like other people: thieves, rogues, adulterers, or even like this tax collector. . . ." Ironically, in Jesus' teaching, the Greek word that we translate to English as "thank" is *eucharisto*. Many churches use that same word to describe the remembering (sacrament or ordinance) of the Lord's Supper. Jesus implicitly makes the point that comparing oneself with others in matters of morality, knowledge, experience, or the quantity or quality of possessions is an unhelpful basis for gratitude. Jesus concludes his teaching with this parable by noting that the "less religious" publican (tax collector) was sincere in acknowledging his sin to God. Such personal honesty before God is the result of an authentic gratitude. Authentic gratitude is feeling grateful to God not for what one has or for what has positively developed to prop up our personal desires, but feeling grateful for who God is: the Lord of heaven and earth, the One who is both just and merciful. That's how disciples across the centuries gather as "church" and celebrate the Eucharist, the "meal" of bread and wine (or grape juice) that indicates thanks to God for God becoming known and giving new life through the birth, life, ministry, death, and resurrection of Jesus.

Post 4. "I Can't Outgive God."[2] Your Gratia-graph grows when the pinball hits this post because you have realized that God's giving grace (holy justice and mercy) to God's people is a giving that cannot be matched. One need never be too conservative or reserved with gratitude if gratitude is based on one's relationship with God.

In another parable from the Gospel according to Luke (15:11–32), which we explored in chapter 3, the "elder brother," who also was the "conservative brother" (who could be an elder and conservative sister), complains to the parent who is throwing a lavish party in celebration of the return of the younger (wasteful and "prodigal") brother (who could be a younger and "prodigal" sister). The more responsible and conservative son (or daughter) protests that the celebrating father (or mother) never threw a party for him (or her) and his (or her) friends. The parent replies, ". . . you are always with me, and all that is mine is yours. But we had to celebrate and rejoice, because this brother of yours was dead and has come to life; he was lost and has been found."

If the lavishly giving, party-throwing parent symbolizes God, then certainly "I/we can't outgive God." God's grace is lavish and liberally given, even prodigally spent. God's grace is given and spent even on the prodigal and wasteful children for whose return home God awaits with love. ("Home," of course, is no particular geographic location, but rather a healthy relationship of abiding love, appreciation, and respect.)

In another biblical story (1 Kgs. 17:8–16), a single parent, who happens to be a widow, is attempting to care for her son during a devastating drought and resulting famine. Her situation is as bad or worse than the nursery rhyme of "Mother Hubbard," who went to her "cupboard to get her poor dog a bone" and found the cupboard utterly empty. When the faithful prophet Elijah senses God leading him to the widow's front yard to ask for a piece of cornbread because he too is starving, she, at first, turns him away. He encourages her to risk trusting that God will provide enough oil and meal for the three of them to have a piece of cornbread. As pessimistically as she viewed her plight (and her son's), her change of mind to trust God in this matter of deprivation so that sharing became a possibility indicates that (1) God can be trusted even when our "means" (and possessions) are very meager and (2) "I can't outgive God."

Post 5. "Everything Is Stewardship." Your Gratia-graph grows when the pinball hits this post because you have realized that nothing belongs to any individual. A steward is one who is responsible for some part of life that actually belongs to another.

If convinced of the testimony of various books of the Bible, we can approach life with the understanding that everything belongs to God. God creates, relates to, forgives the failings of, and makes new the lives of human beings, all the while imploring human beings to trust, no matter what happens in life, that God will eternally be God as known through the scriptures and as known through and in Jesus the Christ.

Some persons have said, "Every good gift is a gift given by God." Qualifying this statement somewhat, others have said, "Every good gift is a loan from God." This second perspective, understanding God's gifts as loans, seems more promising than the "gifts as gifts" perspective because accepting a gift, saying "thank you," and feeling that receiving the gift results in ownership is very easy: "You (or someone) gave it to me, so it is now mine." The "gift as gift" perspective actually becomes, "You gave it to me, so now it's mine (or ours)."

Unless we specify that God's gifts are actually loans, human beings begin exercising the privileges of ownership. There's a saying, "Possession is nine-tenths of the law," which means that if you have something in your possession, and especially if you have possessed it for a considerable length of time, a strong presumption exists that the item rightfully and legally belongs to you. The "burden of proof" falls on anyone else who claims some contending right of ownership on that item.

Even if one is not claiming ownership, presumptions of unchecked stewardship veer God's people off course. Genesis 1:28 quoted and "taken to heart" without qualification or reflection creates a presumption of unchecked stewardship.

> God blessed [the male and female of humankind], and God said to
> them, "Be fruitful and multiply, and fill the earth and subdue it;
> and have dominion over the fish of the sea and over the birds of the
> air and over every living thing that moves upon the earth."[3]

The words translated into English as "subdue" and "have dominion" do not grant license to humankind to run rampant over the earth spilling oil, causing the extinction of species, waging war, etc. We do well to remember that God alone holds legal title.[4]

Compared to all the other creatures (from ants to condors to whales) that God pronounced "good," the storytellers of Genesis understand humankind as the high mark or top-of-the-line achievement of God's creative power in process. (Is this because of human beings thinking of ourselves more highly than we think of other creatures? Or do we definitely have more capabilities, brainwise, for self-transcendence and personal evaluation than other creatures?)

As one example, parents are stewards of their children's lives, and parents are accountable to the larger communities of which they and their children are citizens. In many countries, laws make it illegal for parents to abuse children as if children were possessions or property and less than fully human. Similarly, human beings are stewards generally of all the earth. We are accountable always to God. God eternally holds title to the entire "spread"; therefore, we are never given permission to abuse the earth (or outer space) or the earth's creatures and humans, because everything everywhere belongs to God!

Bible teacher and student Walter Brueggemann writes that "subdue" and "have dominion" are callings ("vocations") from God and tasks of responsibility for the human creature. Our vocation, our reason for being, includes "exercising freedom with and authority over all the other creatures." The power God gives to humans for this responsibility is "power exercised as God exercises power . . . power which invites, evokes, and permits . . . (and is never) coercive or tyrannical." Brueggemann notes that exercising or having "dominion" is like a faithful, conscientious shepherd who "cares for, tends, and feeds" those for whom the shepherd is responsible. No exploitation, manipulation, or greed rightly enters the picture—not in the relationships of parents and children, not in the relationships of humans with any part of creation.[5]

At this point, you may be thinking: This accountability and responsibility stuff sounds like more of a "have to, ought, and should" nature than would be related to "gratitude." Didn't we say earlier, "Gratitude that is required will not truly be gratitude for very long, if ever"? We did say that. Do you also remember, though, Immensa Gratia pinball post number 1? God establishes, initiates, and fulfills grace-based relationships with God's people. In other words, the calling to responsible stewardship (communicated through Scripture and God's spirit) grows from our identity as God's children. You might say, "If we are human creatures, we are stewards responsible to God." This relationship of God to human creatures, who are God's stewards, results in a type of wholesome joy not otherwise possible. From that relationship flow the headwaters of a river of gratitude!

In the tradition of many of Israel's faithful prophets, Jesus spoke frequently about human beings as stewards responsible to each other and responsible to God. If everything is stewardship, "everything" includes at least six categories (with subcategories), outlined something like this:

1. Relationships: personal (family, friends, colleagues, strangers, enemies); public (general/"private sector" and political/governmental)
2. Health: personal, public, physical, mental, emotional
3. Economics: personal, local, national, international
4. Ecology: air, land, fresh water, salt water, subsurface, outer space
5. Time: clock, calendar, historical
6. Faith: personal, particular communities and communions, historical, interfaith

In a dot.com world and in the midst of a postmodern ethos, no narrow pattern is available for being a faithful steward of God's gifts loaned to us. No single "answer" or set of answers appears for the complex challenges God's people face in life around the globe and across the centuries.

The following story offers an example of how points of view and human beings interacting, thinking, studying, and exploring may employ different methods as stewards of God. In spite of their differences, however, they each seem to be moving toward an enhanced experience, understanding, and practice of gratitude in the midst of life and world.

The youth of a local church began preparing in January for a youth-led worship service with the entire congregation scheduled for early February. They had decided the theme for worship that Sunday would be "simplicity." As they began their preparations, an article appeared in the local newspaper and became a focus of their discussion.

The article was titled "WWJD: What Would Jesus Drive?"[6] The title's roots can be traced to the initials on a popular bracelet during the 1990s worn by children, teens, and some adults. "WWJD" printed on the bracelets represented both an ethical question and a perceived basis for decision making in a given situation or dilemma, "What would Jesus do?"

Reporting on concerns raised about the environmental impact of so-called sport-utility vehicles (SUVs), the writer mentioned a group by the name of Religious Witness of the Earth (RWE). RWE opposes automakers' building SUVs and consumers' purchasing and leasing them to drive. This group and others are concerned about SUVs and any vehicles or energy-consuming industries with excessively high fossil-fuel needs leading to increased emissions and pollution.[7]

One opponent of SUVs has said, "My hope is that people won't check their faith at the door of these car dealerships. Our churches and synagogues and mosques are the only places left in our society that can posit some goal other than the accumulation for our existence here on earth." This conviction led to the almost tongue-in-cheek question: "What would Jesus drive?" (Someone, obviously well aware of the limited options of Jesus' own day and time, has answered: "A donkey.")[8]

While not directly disagreeing with the concerned citizens or with the writer of the article, the youth who were planning that worship service went in a somewhat different direction and came out in a slightly different place. The Gospel proclamation by two of the youth raised the question of vehicle cost and the issue of social status. After reading Jesus' words from Matthew 6:24–34, one of the youth suggested that (1) obligating oneself to pay high costs for purchase and maintenance and (2) attempting to enhance one's social standing by the model of vehicle one drives or by the brand of clothes one wears leads to personal and budgetary pressures and worries. Jesus teaches that disciples then and now can choose to avoid exactly these sorts of worries.[9]

The second youth read from 1 Timothy 6:6–10 and suggested that if it's true "we bring nothing into this world and can take nothing out of it," then possessing money and using money to help people is positive, while loving money is negative. The second youth then said: "Is it even helpful to ask, 'What would Jesus drive?'?" (because that's no choice Jesus ever had to face) and "If the love of money is the root of all evil, what does the plant look like that grows out of the root? Will it always be an ugly sight?" (1 Tim. 6:10). After a quote from American writer Charles Warner— "Simplicity is making the journey of this life with just baggage enough"[10]—the youth concluded with these words: "Simplicity does not mean that there are not complications in your life or hard decisions, but being focused on what is most important to God all through the years."[11]

These two youth felt no need either to issue a blanket condemnation of all who drive SUVs or to issue a condemnation of the personalized license plate seen on a late-model Mercedes-Benz sedan ("I B VAIN"). Instead, they chose to explore how certain teachings of Jesus and the early church "make sense" for life and decision making in our different time and culture. As stated earlier, when interacting, thinking, studying, and exploring, persons may employ different methods as stewards of God. In spite of their slight differences with the persons quoted in the newspaper article, those two teen church members seem to be moving toward an enhanced experience, understanding, and practice of gratitude in the midst of life and world. Convinced that our identity is rooted in God's relationship with us rather than in what we have or accomplish, the two suggested in their preaching exactly what Immensa Gratia's fifth pinball post suggests: "Everything is stewardship."

How eccentric are we becoming by the grace of God? Possibly the most eccentric proposal of all is Immensa Gratia's sixth pinball post.

Post 6. "Joyful gratitude possible when much is very negative." Your Gratia-graph grows when the pinball hits this post because you have realized that joyful gratitude is possible in the relationship with God, even when much is very negative in life.

How can one possibly be grateful to God when bombs are exploding close by; when chemotherapy drugs are searing into one's body through a tube and needle; when the bank account is lower than the bills to be paid; when failure, rejection, and grief seem to cascade and pile one upon the other?

Looking to the Bible, the prophet Habakkuk never gave glib or frivolous advice to anyone. Job, as a character in the book that carries his name, never gave or accepted suggestions that discounted tremendous grief and agony, whether physical, emotional, or spiritual.

Certain traditions of faith interpretation in the history of both Israel and the church suggest that bad things happen when God is displeased with particular sins of human beings. Another tradition, though, exemplified by Ecclesiastes, Job, and in certain teachings of Jesus, never explains tragedy and devastation based on a rationale that God causes particular horrendous adversities which persons periodically experience in life. Their interpretive strand in the biblical tradition basically says, "Human beings are sinners. Bad things happen, including suffering and death, sometimes related to human sin. Never, though, should one believe that every bad development is God's punishment for some particular sin, whether known and identified or unrealized and yet to be identified."

The closing verses of the book of the prophet Habakkuk (3:17–19) offer a testimony of faith and gratitude (even joyful gratitude!) that may be unsurpassed, given the desperate circumstances described:

> Though the fig tree does not blossom,
> and no fruit is on the vines;
> though the produce of the olive fails
> and the fields yield no food;
> though the flock is cut off from the fold
> and there is no herd in the stalls,
> yet will I rejoice in the LORD;

I will exult in the God of my salvation.
God, the Lord, is my strength;
he makes my feet like the feet of a deer,
and makes me tread upon the heights.

For many years, the story has been told of an experiment undertaken by a group of psychologists. Supposedly two children, each six years old, were given a small shovel and placed in separate rooms piled high with horse manure. After half an hour, the videotape of the experiment indicated that one child began to cry and whine for someone to open the door. The other child appeared to be whispering something while digging with passion into the center of the manure pile. When the volume on the audio was turned up, the scientists could hear the whispers. Over and over the child was saying, "There's got to be a pony in here somewhere!"

Obviously, this story illustrates opposite reactions to adverse situations. One child almost instinctively (and enthusiastically) tries to discover unseen possibilities. The other as quickly asks for the seemingly pointless and miserable experiment to end and for the door to be opened.

Immensa Gratia post number six, however, is not about the pony that might or might not be buried under the pile of manure; nor is the post about an attitude of optimism being superior to pessimism when one's situation in life stinks. Scripture encourages honest communication between God's people and God in prayer: telling God how bad life is! (Think about Jesus praying from the cross as he suffered there, quoting from Ps. 22: "My God, my God, why have you forsaken me?")

Scripture also encourages honest communication when relationships between persons are broken or damaged, with a goal of increasing health in those relationships. If matters are negative, recognizing the degree to which they are negative, engaging in prayer and conversation, and seeking relief in any ways possible and appropriate are positive for increasing the health and wholeness that God always desires.

At the center of God's eccentric grace (yielding gratitude), though, is the steadfast relationship of God with God's people. Persons across the centuries report experiences of that steadfast relationship, creating within them a trust in God's presence that continues and abides even in the midst of suffering. People suffer and die from war, disease, famine, storms, accidents, terrorism, and violent, abusive behavior. Jesus taught that, in such situations, the Lord of heaven and earth is mysteriously present with those who are suffering, even though one may legitimately wonder, "Where is God in the hell of this experience?"

John Milbank has argued that religious teachings promoting how Jesus died as a sacrifice for the sin of the world are not nearly as helpful and convincing to him as the understanding that Jesus was crucified as "trash"![12] Milbank's thoughts are consistent with a significant strand in the Gospel accounts suggesting that certain officials of established religious and governmental institutions detested and sought to quash Jesus' ministry and teachings. They wanted him trashed and made it happen. The love of God that Jesus represented and embodied was rejected, snuffed, and discarded by persons who were more interested in preserving the status quo than in God's love.

We never need to pray for adversity or suffering, but no individual or group of persons, according to Jesus and the biblical story and teachings as a whole, ever experiences healing by pledging allegiance to ways of thinking and living that seek prosperity and advancement. Those ways and thinking only exclude others and show no concern for the ones left behind in the dust. That's why the apostle Paul, when teaching about God's radical love known in and through Jesus, concludes chapter 12 of 1 Corinthians and introduces chapter 13 with the transition sentence, ". . . I will show you a still more excellent way."

That more excellent way is the way of God's eccentric grace transforming all of God's people, for which we can be grateful even in the most devastating of circumstances. Not even death has the last word in the presence of God's eternal, mysterious, steadfast love.

Willie Morris's novel *Taps*, published after the author's death, tells the coming-of-age story of a young man (Swayze Barksdale) in a small town in northwest Mississippi during the early 1950s. The book's title derives from Swayze's often repeated experience as a trumpeter hired to play "Taps" at the graveside of soldiers from that area who had been killed in Korea and brought home for burial. In telling his tale, Swayze looks back from the vantage point of his adult years to revisit relationships and events in that community which developed in him a gratitude for love that never ends, even through heart-rending trauma and grief.[13]

In another book, *A Rock and a Hard Place*, Anthony ("Tony") Godby Johnson recounts the deprivation, beatings, and sexual abuse he endured from his birth parents, his life on the streets of New York City fleeing that situation, his suicidal despair, and the care he found at last from others, prior to being diagnosed with AIDS. At the conclusion of his autobiography, this remarkable teen writes:

> At the moment of my death, I want three things. I want not to be afraid. I want the people I love to know just how much I love them,

and that a part of me will be inside them and make them smile every time they think about me. . . . Most important, I want to know that I have done everything that was humanly possible to contribute to my world in some kind of way. I want to give back in gratitude for having been able to be here. . . . [14]

Tony's approach to life bangs the sixth post of the Immensa Gratia pinball machine until its bells and lights wear out: "Joyful gratitude possible when much is very negative."

John Calvin, of early and mid-sixteenth-century Europe, had his personal seal designed with the illustration of an open human hand holding a heart aflame. Surrounding that illustration was the Latin phrase, "*Cor meum tibi offero Domine prompte et sincere*" ("My heart to you I offer, Lord, promptly and sincerely").[15]

As hard as life can be, the only way we can consistently (and eccentrically) make that offering is from a faith and trust that God, by grace, always gives more than we can ever imagine. This giving, of course, occurs in, through, and beyond all human suffering. It's the only way gratitude with joy is continually possible.

NOTES AND JOURNALING OPPORTUNITIES

I.   Parts of this chapter with which I have mostly agreed in the past:

II. Parts of this chapter with which I have mostly disagreed in the past:

III. Parts of this chapter which have presented new thoughts or information for me:

IV. What's in this chapter . . .

(a) prompts me to remember

(b) prompts me, from years past, to wonder about

(c) prompts me to want to ask, to investigate, to research

(d) prompts me to wonder about changing

(e) prompts me to wonder about the near future in the following ways

(f) prompts me to wonder about the more distant future in the following ways

V. Personal writings, sketches, drawings related to this chapter

Am I My Siblings' Keeper, or Are They the Weakest Links?

Community in a Survivor's World

"It's time again to vote off another member. Cast your vote for the weakest link. Who will it be?"
—Lines similar to those from the game shows *Survivor* and *The Weakest Link*

In the Dallas suburb of Mesquite, Texas, in the mid-1970s, Alex was playing junior-high football before a packed crowd (about a hundred or so). Alex loved football and he had a dream. This dream was to score a touchdown because he knew if he did, his name would be announced over the PA system. "On the touchdown, number thirteen, Alex Thornburg!" Everyone in the stands would know who he was and would cheer his great accomplishment. To hear his name over the PA system was to be recognized and considered special in the eyes of all who witnessed this triumph. The problem was that as a wide receiver, he never had the chance to touch the football. In junior high, they had trouble handing off, much less throwing the ball, so Alex was a glorified blocker who would run out when the ball was hiked and try to get in someone's way. His dream of hearing his name announced seemed destined never to happen.

Then came that fateful afternoon when the quarterback in the huddle called for a reverse. For those less familiar with the arcane language of football, a reverse is where the quarterback takes the ball and runs toward one side of the field. The receiver fakes upfield and then reverses his pattern and begins to run toward the quarterback, whereupon the quarterback hands him the ball. Hopefully the defense has been fooled and chases the quarterback so that the receiver can then have a free field in which to run.

Alex was beyond excited when he heard the play called in the huddle and couldn't even feel his legs as he lined up on one side of the field. His chance had come to accomplish his dream and hear over the PA system those magic words, "On the touchdown, number thirteen, Alex Thornburg." Everyone would know who he was. Alex tried to look nonchalant as he lined up and the ball was hiked. He faked a step forward and reversed his field and began running toward the quarterback who was running toward him, and before he knew it the ball was in his hands.

It had worked! The defense was chasing the quarterback and Alex had an open field with nothing in sight except the goal line. He could walk right in and score the touchdown. His dream was at hand. He would be dancing in the end zone and soon everyone would know who he was: "On the touchdown, number thirteen, Alex Thornburg!" The moment was incredible.

He planted his foot and stepped upfield to enter his glory when . . . he dropped the ball. To this day, Alex does not know how he dropped the ball, but he watched as it bounced across the field into the hands of a rather surprised defensive player. There would be no dancing, no recognition of his great triumph, no crowd to know who he was. As he walked off the field with his head down, through, he heard the PA crackle, "On the fumble, number thirteen, Alex Thornburg." Everyone knew who he was.

A CULTURE OF SELF

Human nature wants to be recognized, to be seen as special for our accomplishments, to score the touchdown and hear the crowd cheer. We want to dance in the end zone so others can see us and cheer us and know who we are. One has only to turn on shows like *The Jerry Springer Show* to see the lengths people will go to be seen on TV. (If invited, Thornburg and Foote might be tempted to accept for a Springer theme like "Presbyterian Ministers at Each Others' Throats!") Even if we would never say it out loud, most of us wish in some form or another to hear our names announced over the PA system.

Why is this recognition so important to us? In part it is life in the twenty-first century. Our culture celebrates the self. In the words of a popular TV psychologist, *Self Matters*.[1] In a culture of self we spend a lot of time with self-promotion, self-growth, self-development, and self-help.

One has only to peruse the aisles of any bookstore to see all the books that are available to help us fix ourselves or let us be ourselves. Look at the progression of popular magazines over the past few years that have gone from *People*, to *Us*, and finally now to *Self* magazine. The self appears to have become the be-all and end-all of life. One wonders about the possibility that we might grow sick of ourselves.

In this culture of self, self-absorption is encouraged. We spend most of our energy to satisfy ourselves, and we invest much of our energy for our own self-satisfaction. Work is understood not in the context of contributing to societal good, but as a means to achieve financial rewards for the particular self or family. College students typically do not choose careers in a sense of vocation or calling, but in terms of the salary they can make. We take this self-absorption so much for granted that it goes unquestioned.

This self-focus infiltrates all aspects of our daily life. People leave marriages because the relationship no longer meets their needs, or because their spouse doesn't make them happy anymore. Some parents even have children because as parents they feel it completes themselves, or so they can live their lives through their children. We pay taxes not for the good of society but for what the government and other state institutions can do for us. Our desire to have more and more for ourselves threatens the fragile ecology of this planet.

Unless we think the self does not play an important role in our own theological reflection, let us ask how much of popular faith is self-absorbed. Salvation is perceived in individualistic terms, where we worry over our particular soul's destination. Our relationship with Jesus Christ is understood as a personal relationship. Spirituality is about self-actualization and personal happiness, and participation in the church is based on how that church meets our needs and the needs of our family. We act as if the church exists simply for our particular selves. Faith in our dot.com world has simply become a form of spiritual navel-gazing.

This preoccupation with the self has had a dire effect on our understanding of the meaning of community. In fact, because of this culture of self we are not quite sure what "community" means. In 1985, Robert Bellah and several colleagues published a groundbreaking social survey in which they noted this loss of the meaning of community.[2] He tells of countless interviews with individuals who do not have a common language of community. They wrestle with what that word means in the context of a society so dependent upon individualism. Bellah challenges our society to recover the language of community, for our very survival is dependent on that recovery. We spend the rest of this chapter discussing the third e.i., community.

COMMUNITY IN A SURVIVOR'S WORLD

The TV reality show *Survivor* has been a huge success, with some of the highest ratings among all programs. At the time of this writing, four successful competitions have been broadcast and a fifth is in the works. The program follows a group of people in an isolated location—a rainforest, a desert, an island—as they try to outsmart, outlast, and outplay each other for $1 million. *Survivor* serves as an interesting metaphor for how our culture understands and shapes its language about community.

First, the sole purpose of this pseudocommunity is to win $1 million. While most people would not perceive community in our society for this reason (though it may be argued otherwise), the purpose is still to use community to achieve some personal individualistic ends. We see community as existing to meet our needs, whether they are material, relational, or spiritual. Community's purpose is to satisfy the needs of an individual. (One wonders if a rule prohibits the participants in the show from simply agreeing that they all will share in $1 million. This result would seem a more appealing option for all participants, as no one goes away empty-handed.) Community is less understood as cooperation than a competition of individuals over finite resources. We then participate in those groups that better serve those ends. Community is less a blessing to be celebrated than a means to a particular end for selfish reasons.

Second, the false community of *Survivor* understands that one must eliminate the most disagreeable and threatening people. On the show, community members vote off other players because they rub them the wrong way, or they see them as a threat to achieving their own goal of winning, or simply because they just don't like them. We see the same kind of behavior in communities in our society. We tend to understand community as connecting people who are like-minded or who hold the same values that we do. We also seek out people simply because they look like us. Those people who disagree with our viewpoints, who have the audacity to contradict our values, are not considered part of our community. To "vote them off the island" is perfectly acceptable. Those people we find threatening are especially to be pushed outside our sense of community. Community is understood to be exclusive of those who do not fit within our particular needs or values.

Third, in the strange sense of community in *Survivor,* alliances are formed to compete with each other for the final prize.[3] These alliances develop between participants as protection and insurance that they will survive the game. Despite the conflict and backbiting inherent in such a game, these alliances prove rather effective in accomplishing the goals of its members. Some recruiting takes place to strengthen one's own alliance, with secret conversations and arguments concerning perceived loyalty or betrayal. In many ways, communities in our society shape themselves in this fashion as well. We use the very language of community to define ourselves as part of a particular alliance, whether it be the Euro American community, African American community, Mexican American community, gay and lesbian community, or even a political party. Not surprisingly, these alliances have proven effective in achieving results for their particular constituencies, and criticism is heaped upon people who are understood to betray the needs and goals of these alliances. The language of community has become identification with a particular alliance seeking to compete with others for the good of its members.

The dynamics of community in *Survivor* result in people trying not to be different. Competitors describe trying to lay low so that they do not stand out and become noticed. They remain as unobtrusive and compliant as possible in order to stay off other people's radar screens and not be voted off the island. In other words, eccentricity is discouraged in a *Survivor's* world because it will only land you in trouble. Someone who is in the least bit different or disagrees with the group becomes a target for being voted off the competition. Much in the same way, eccentricity is discouraged in a dot.com world, where to be truly different and in disagreement with pseudocommunities is to be ostracized and pushed out. One wonders again if the eccentric are disappearing from the world because communities' purpose is to rid themselves of such eccentricity.

As with any generalizations, oversimplifying the metaphor of *Survivor* for our understanding of community can be dangerous, but noting the similarities between our culture's use of community and the reality TV show is utterly fascinating. *Survivor* may be more "real" than we would like to admit. This reality shapes even the church's understanding of community as defined by *Survivor*. The church becomes a means to an end, a structure defined by meeting the needs of the individuals within it. If the church ceases to meet those needs, participants leave to go to other churches that can be more responsive to their needs. Churches often see themselves in competition for a dwindling number of resources (people) and define success according to the size of one's congregation, one's building, or one's budget (the three Bs again, first mentioned in chapter 3). We must ask ourselves as a church whether this definition of community as a means to accomplish an end truly is the community of God's people.

Church in the ethos of our culture also values sameness. A school of thought in evangelism as recruitment holds that churches will grow if they seek out people who reflect similar ethnicity, socioeconomic backgrounds, and like-minded values. The truth is that many people find such churches attractive for the safety and comfort of being with others who look, think, and act just like we do. When individuals within a church raise conflicting viewpoints, the tendency is to push them out to the edges so their voices may be muted. In a dot.com world, churches attempt to show a homogeneous front at the expense of differing voices.

The church of today reflects a conglomerate of alliances articulating their particular theological points of view in conflict with each other. These alliances understand themselves to be in competition to sway the larger institution in a particular direction. More than a little backbiting and gossiping go on as each alliance strives to win the final prize. What that final prize may be is unclear, but community as defined in this way simply understands itself to be a special-interest group.

Community in a *Survivor's* world is structured on these assumptions. Community exists as a means of achieving goals for the individual participants, community is a group of like-minded people, and community is a conglomerate of alliances in competition with each other. The challenge to this ethos can be found in the gospel, where community is defined in quite a different way.

THE ECCENTRICITY OF COMMUNITY

In Luke 10:25–37, we are told of an encounter between Jesus and an expert in the law. The lawyer stands up to test Jesus and asks, "What must I do to inherit eternal life?" Not an easy question! Jesus responds as he does many times with a question of his own. (Socrates would have been proud.) "What is written in the law? What do you read there?" (Luke 10:26). The lawyer gives an astute answer, reciting from Deuteronomy and Leviticus the passages to love the Lord your God with all your heart, soul, strength, and mind, and to love your neighbor as yourself. This expert knows his stuff and has the theology right. Jesus tells him he got it correct and reminds him to act on what he has said. Jesus was big on not simply having the right theology but actually living it out in everyday life.

But then an interesting dialogue takes place as the lawyer wants more from Jesus. Luke tells us the man wanted to justify himself and therefore asks, "Who is my neighbor?" (Luke 10:29). Note that the expert in the law has framed all his questions around concerns for himself. "What must I do to inherit eternal life?" "How may I be justified?" He would fit right in with our culture, which frames religious reflections around the self. You cannot help but notice the self-absorption of the man who knows the law. His very questions reflect his self-concern for the condition of his own soul, which is his version of spiritual navel-gazing.

Jesus responds with a story, not surprising since storytelling is his eccentric style of teaching. The story begins with a man going down from Jerusalem to Jericho where he falls into the hands of robbers who strip him, beat him, and leave him half dead on the side of the road. Now the first person to walk by is a priest, who passes by on the other side of the road. Then along comes a Levite, who also passes by on the other side of the road. Jesus doesn't tell us why the priest and the Levite do not stop to aid the injured man. Many scholars make suppositions about their motivations in passing by: The priest and Levite were avoiding being defiled because of strict laws that restricted religious authorities from touching someone dead (or who appeared to be dead); or the priest and Levite were simply in too much of a hurry doing their sacred business to pause and aid the victim. Whatever reason we ascribe to their seemingly callous behavior, one point is clear. In most cases, the failure to respond to human need is shaped by self-absorption, whether for religious or personal reasons. Whatever motivations we imagine for the Levite and the priest, inevitably they are reasons that are self-focused in nature (purity, busyness, or simple indifference).

But then along comes a Samaritan. He sees the injured man and is moved with pity (the Greek word here could also mean compassion). The Samaritan goes to him and bandages his wounds, puts him on his own animal and brings him to an inn. He pays the innkeeper and promises to return to pay more if needed. Obviously Jesus has drawn a dramatic contrast between the priest and Levite and the Samaritan. This difference would have been a scandal for the Palestinian Jews who listened to the story. The priest and Levite were highly respected representatives of the religious establishment and society. They held positions of authority and privilege. The Samaritan on the other hand was despised and shunned by proper Jewish society. The prejudice between Samaritans and the Palestinian Jews, like most prejudice, is hard for us to comprehend out of context, but suffice it to say that Samaritans were seen by the ordinary Jews as subversive, divisive, heretical, and as enemies. They just didn't like each other.

Jesus' portrayal of the Samaritan instead of the more "moral" people (at least in the minds of the listeners) responding to human need is troublesome. When Jesus asks the lawyer who was the neighbor to the man who fell among thieves, the lawyer cannot even say "Samaritan." "The one who showed him mercy" (Luke 10:37). The lawyer finds it hard to swallow this parable and its ramifications. Here the lawyer wanted guidance about justifying himself, and Jesus tells a story that calls into question certain assumptions about what that means. Jesus has moved the question away from self-justification to another issue entirely, the question of neighbor and community.

Seeing this parable as a simple moral teaching on prejudice and being a good neighbor would be easy, but within the context of the lawyer's search for salvation the story becomes a commentary on the nature of community as Jesus sees it. Former boundaries and barriers between people, which defined communities according to static and traditional ways, no longer apply. Instead of defining community in terms of purity and opposition to disagreeable elements, community becomes the place where compassion and mercy meet.

You could even say the lawyer had it wrong, even in the end. The real neighbor in this story is not solely the Samaritan but the man who fell among thieves, or, for that matter, anyone who is in need. The neighbor and thus the community became known in compassionate engagement with the "other," the poor sap who has been stripped, beaten, and left for dead. What Jesus has done in telling this story in response to our legal expert's questions is shift attention away from the lawyer's self-focus to the other. The lawyer knew the law, probably obeyed the law, and was religiously correct in all ways, so he may be justified. The lawyer, though, didn't understand that the spiritual life is not about our own justification, but about the gift of the other.

THE GIFT OF THE OTHER

The radical nature of the gospel is the call to embrace the "other." In Jesus Christ we have one who taught by his life and his words a life lived not for self but for the other. The early church understood even the incarnation as Christ who came not to rule but to serve. The whole of Jesus' life is a testament to loving the other, from his breaking bread with undesirables like tax collectors and prostitutes to healing the artificial divisions that human society creates. His teachings stressed a life lived in love of neighbor, even when that neighbor would be considered an enemy. His crucifixion represented the ultimate expression of sacrificial love even for the ones who nailed him on the cross. One cannot read the Gospels without being struck by the strangeness and challenge of a life lived for the other.

The nature of community in the New Testament reflects this focus on the other. When the disciples begin to argue among themselves about who will sit next to Jesus in the kingdom to come, Jesus speaks of true discipleship as servanthood to the other. According to John, on the final night of his life, Jesus shows the disciples the meaning of community by washing their feet and commanding them to do likewise (John 13:1–17). Paul is constantly reminding the churches he has planted of an ethic of "one anothering." Love one another, serve one another, pray for one another. In fact, the other is a gift to be cherished and celebrated, for in this gift we encounter Jesus Christ. The language and image of community as other-directed is a far cry from the culture of self we live in today.

Community as the gift of the other is not simply concerned with achieving goals for the self. Community is not a means to an end but a gift in and of itself. We do not simply choose the community of Christ to participate in, but we are called and blessed into this community. What a radical notion to understand that church membership is not simply a personal preference, but a calling into a particular community. We do not choose God as much as God chooses us.

If community is an essential indicator of grace, a gift given in its fullness by God to us, then we cannot reject the undesirable or disagreeable. If the other, especially the other whom we might not like, is given to us, then we are called to cherish the gift. Jesus didn't command us to like everyone as much as we are called to love the other. (Every married couple understands the difference, as on some days you don't particularly like your spouse, but you still love them.) The other then is not seen as an issue to resolve or a problem to overcome but rather a gift to be celebrated. This gift of others in all their strengths and weakness, in all their cantankerous and irritating points of view, should be celebrated and loved.

Finally, Christian community does not advocate changing the other into an image of ourselves or convincing them of the rightness of our views. Community is not an alliance where others must be recruited and argued into submission. Community is by its very nature a diversity of people, a plethora of opinions, and a conglomeration of strange blessings. Like all gifts, community should be nurtured and cherished, not conquered and brow-beaten.

AM I MY BROTHER'S (AND SISTER'S) KEEPER?

In the movie *Grand Canyon*,[4] the scattered lives of various people in modern-day Los Angeles are explored. The movie begins with Mack, an upper-class businessman, driving home from a Lakers' basketball game when he takes the wrong turn into the wrong neighborhood and, at this inopportune time, his car engine quits. He hurriedly calls for a tow truck, but before it could arrive he finds his life threatened by a gang of teenagers. He is saved by the timely arrival of Simon, a working-class black man, who brings the tow truck. Out of this chance encounter an unlikely friendship begins as the movie traces the lives of these two very different men and their families. Mack's wife, Claire, in another chance encounter, discovers an abandoned baby in a park. She wants to apply to adopt the baby. Mack is less sure, and in a pivotal scene Claire challenges Mack to see these chance encounters as miracles, gifts from God. How do we know that these aren't miracles, she asks. How do we know that they aren't gifts given to us in life?

We in the eccentric church are called to see the others as miracles, and these gifts are the basis of our community. For the eccentric church, the other is the miracle given by God. We may not be our brothers' and sisters' keepers, but we are our brother's (or sister's) brother, and we are our brother's (or sister's) sister.[5] Community is the place where we cherish these miracles and are cherished for our own uniqueness. Nothing is more eccentric in a *Survivor*'s world than to be more concerned with the survival of others than with the survival of our own souls.

NOTES AND JOURNALING OPPORTUNITIES

I.   Parts of this chapter with which I have mostly agreed in the past:

II. Parts of this chapter with which I have mostly disagreed in the past:

III. Parts of this chapter which have presented new thoughts or information for me:

IV. What's in this chapter . . .

   (a) prompts me to remember

   (b) prompts me, from years past, to wonder about

   (c) prompts me to want to ask, to investigate, to research

   (d) prompts me to wonder about changing

   (e) prompts me to wonder about the near future in the following ways

   (f) prompts me to wonder about the more distant future in the following ways

V. Personal writings, sketches, drawings related to this chapter

"Have It Your Way" or "We Love to See You Smile"?

Courage in a Fast-Food World

> *"Courage is grace under pressure."*
> —John F. Kennedy,
> quoting Ernest Hemingway[1]

The citizens of the small French village of Le Chambon-sur-Lignon saved the lives of countless Jewish refugees during the Nazi occupation and the Vichy government's collaboration by hiding them from the authorities, sometimes for more than four years,[2] despite the clear danger to their lives and homes. Led by their pastor Andre Trocme, and committed to Christian nonviolence, they welcomed Jewish refugees hiding from the horrors of the Holocaust.

Where other communities in France and, especially, in Germany had failed to even lift a finger to aid those poor souls, this small town of meager resources gave of themselves to house, feed, and succor the Jews. Some citizens were imprisoned and even killed because of their actions. Their example has brought many to ask the why and how of their risking their lives when so many in that dark time refused to even see, much less aid, the people being killed. Many people who have studied and talked with survivors and villagers have come up with theories, psychological and social, to explain their courageous stand: The villagers were descendants of refugees themselves and thus generally more sensitive to the plight of the less fortunate. The citizens who aided the Jews had prior psychological experiences of abandonment as children and thus were more compassionate toward others abandoned by society.

Whatever the reason, the striking aspect of the response of these common, everyday people is their nonchalance about what they did. They didn't think they were doing some great, heroic deed or undertaking a supreme feat of courage. Rooted in their life as a religious community, they saw their acts of compassion as a natural expression of their faith. They did what they did because of who they were. When someone comes to your door, you have the choice to open the door or not. They opened the door.

WHAT IS COURAGE?

In reflecting on the nature of courage, the fourth essential indicator (e.i.) of the presence of grace, we usually think in terms of great acts of heroism in wartime or lives sacrificed to save others. On September 11, 2001, we were struck by the courage of the firefighters and policemen who rushed into the World Trade Center to save lives. These great acts of heroism are to be admired and celebrated, but is courage relegated to a few who perform incredible feats of valor in service to a greater good? Or can courage be something more?

If courage is simply a quality of a few who place themselves in danger in service to humankind, then conversely, we cannot claim courage as part and parcel of our spiritual life. Most of us do not run into burning buildings or throw ourselves upon grenades to show courage and, therefore, do not think of courage as a quality we possess in any great quantity. In fact, we leave it to the professionals rather than understand it to be integral to the faith of the Christian community.

But what does courage really entail? Even the firefighters and police officers who ran up the stairs of the World Trade Center towers on September 11, 2001, would describe their actions not as great acts of heroism, but simply doing their jobs. Courage is less a specific act than a way of life, where you do the job despite the pressures and dangers inherent in the situation. Courage is less a particular action of heroism and more a characteristic or quality of life in a person or community. The villagers in Le Chambon did not think of themselves as heroes as much as their courage was an extension of their faith community. Courage was as much their willingness to not conform to the hatred and violence that surrounded them, to not acquiesce to apathy and ignorance of the pain of their fellow human beings, and to not let the knock on the door go unanswered.

Le Chambon's response to the pain and suffering of fellow human beings was rooted in the practices of their Christian community. In their life and the daily shaping of their community they found the courage to confront the evil around them. Their faith practices resulted in their acts of courage, their life together that flowed into acts of heroism. The courageous villagers of Le Chambon acted the way they did because it was who they were as shaped by their life together. Their practices of faith made them different.

Much as a baseball player must practice swinging the bat over and over again, hitting ball after ball to teach the body the rhythm of a perfect swing, we too must practice the faith to learn the rhythm of courage. A baseball player cannot step up to the plate to hit a home run without practicing the swing. In the same way, the villagers of Le Chambon didn't do great acts of courage without the practices that shaped their daily lives. They had already learned by their practices how to hit the home run when it came time. This practicing in everyday life enabled them to see and be different in the world than the surrounding culture. They practiced grace, so when the time of great pressure came, they could exhibit an admirable courage.

Understanding courage in this way, we then come to the crux of the nature of courage for the Christian community: while heroism might show itself in dramatic ways, such as the example of the acts of a community like Le Chambon, at its root it is the community willing to question and challenge the assumptions of the surrounding ethos of the culture. Courage is needed to challenge a mob mentality. Courage is needed to call into question some of the accepted views of how the world is supposed to work. To be eccentric takes courage, particularly in our very conformist society.

A FAST-FOOD CULTURE

Let us take a little detour. One peculiar aspect of our culture in the twenty-first century is that, while there is a passing nod to diversity, in many ways our communities look more and more the same. Some people describe the phenomenon as the "malling" of America, in that the proliferation of shopping centers looks very much the same in Tulsa, Oklahoma, as in Los Angeles, California; Indianapolis, Indiana; or Charlotte, North Carolina. These shopping malls are lined up with chain stores so that in any community you can find a Wal-Mart right next to Home Depot, or a Target right next to Lowe's. This sameness reflects a conformity in our culture that is subtle and often unexamined.

George Ritzer, in his book *The McDonaldization of Society,* describes the "process by which the principles of the fast-food restaurant are coming to dominate more and more sectors of American society as well as of the rest of the world."[3] While not having any particular dislike of McDonald's, Ritzer uses the chain restaurant as a "paradigm case" for describing the ways in which many parts of our society shape life in conformity to its principles. While we may think of our society as diverse and its people as independent, in reality, more and more aspects of our lives reflect a uniform McDonaldized world. Ritzer ascribes the reasons for this McDonaldization to a number of underlying principles that our culture values. Fast-food restaurants are efficient and calculable.[4] They provide service in as efficient a way as possible within the least amount of time. All we have to do is drive through and order our Value Meal, and we can munch on our Big Macs as we are motoring to where we need to go. We can see this celebration of efficiency from Lens Crafters, which promises glasses in an hour, or Jiffy Lube, which can change your oil in fifteen minutes. Part of this efficiency is the comfort of knowing the experience will be the same wherever you go. The process is predictable in that we know it will take this amount of time to receive the same amount of food.[5] Surprises are few when it comes to McDonald's. In a fast-food culture that believes time is money, having one's needs met in as efficient and predictable a manner as possible is highly valued.

Besides this efficiency, a fast-food culture favors quantity over quality. We want more bang for our buck where we can get the biggie size for only a few cents more. Also, while the food isn't necessarily great, at least we will get a lot of it. At the Payless shoe store we can buy two pairs of shoes for the price of one, and at Mazzio's we can get all we can eat. In a fast-food world, quality may be sacrificed at the altar of quantity.

Ritzer points out that this McDonaldization, while rational, results in a monolithic culture in which sameness and comfort replace the human potential.[6] Creativity, thoughtfulness, and humanity are diminished as the culture views everyone as consumers looking for the most efficient, predictable, and calculated experience possible. Ritzer wonders what the world would look like if it were less chained to a homogenized worldview. Are we becoming less human in an effort to be efficient and predictable?

CHURCH IN A FAST-FOOD CULTURE

So, you ask, what's wrong with efficiency and predictability? What does McDonaldization have to do with courage? After all, we two scatter-brained preachers would admit we sometimes take leaps of thought that defy logic, but we would argue that these principles underlying our conforming culture are important because the church has adopted them as its own. In fact, courage for the church in the twenty-first century has much to do with faith practices that challenge this McDonaldization of our humanity. Bear with us as we strive to make the connections.

The church today strives for efficiency and calculability. Who hasn't heard in a board meeting the need for the church to be run like a business, thus implying the need for efficiency? What church doesn't have for numbers a fascination bordering on the fanatical as we calculate membership rolls and worship attendance? How many preachers have heard the complaint that worship went over the requisite hour, or that crying babies disturbed the comfort of the worship experience? For the many churches using a bulletin of worship, God forbid you stray from the predictable liturgy!

The point is that the qualities of efficiency and predictability have become incorporated into the church's functional principles. The result is a less human church, a less compassionate place where people are engaged more as consumers and less as human beings, and where value is placed on the quantity of people rather than the quality of relationships. The challenge for the eccentric church in this strange new world is to be inefficient and unpredictable!

THE COURAGE TO BE INEFFICIENT

Jesus was rather inefficient. He called together a motley crew of disciples without using an organizational chart to gauge each person's effectiveness and skills. Jesus wasted a lot of time with undesirables, eating and drinking so much that he was accused by some of being a lush. What's more, if Jesus was concerned about the numbers of people who followed him, he should have called more than the twelve, who ended up abandoning him anyway. One cannot read the Gospels without being struck by Jesus' eccentricity even in a culture not known for being busy. How much more eccentric he appears in our fast-food culture.

Does the church have the courage to be eccentric in a fast-food world? Do we have the strength to be different in a world looking more and more the same? If courage is more a reflection of our faith practices than individual acts of heroism, what are those practices in light of the McDonaldization of our society? Every Christian community needs to ask itself this question as it examines its culpability and acquiescence to our homogenized world.

One eccentric practice of the church is its worship. Worship is an inefficient use of time and resources. Worship does not exist simply so the community can gather together, nor does it exist to meet our emotional needs. A professional person knowledgeable about ministry and church practices once pointed out, tongue in cheek (sort of!), that worship is a "royal waste of time."[7] In weekly worship the community gathers in silence, song, prayer, and Scripture reading so that we may be shaped to a different rhythm of life, a more human one. In "wasting time" with God, we come to be different from the fast-food world around us.

Other eccentric practices are baptism and the Lord's Supper. In baptism, we are claimed by God and therefore know to whom we belong. Baptism is a political act in that we discover ourselves to be part of a kingdom not of this world. Baptism is God's act through the church whereby a child or an adult is made part of the community, not because they fit a particular mold or model. God claims who God will as God's own, and you never can predict whom God will call. In the same way, the Lord's Supper is a practice of the community where all false divisions and barriers are stripped away. In the Lord's Supper, for that moment, we have a reflection of the true nature of what it means to be a human community. Jesus invites everyone to that table whether they have the same color of skin or hold to the same creeds, and the scary thing is that you cannot predict who will show up at the table.

Many and varied practices of faith make us eccentric. Every faith community has them, and they are as varied as the churches in which they are found. The practice of Bible study exposes us to a different world and a different way of seeing the world. The confession of sin as a practice can bring home our common shared humanity with others as we all rely upon the grace of God. Intentional welcoming of strangers reminds us that Jesus can show up in many different ways. The practice of service in all its forms reminds us that we live not for ourselves but for others. All these practices make us into a different people, eccentric in a conforming culture.

To think of those everyday activities as being acts of courage may seem strange. But particularly in our McDonaldized world, our conformist culture, these everyday activities shape us into eccentricity. These activities are truly courageous acts, although some people may find them inefficient uses of time and not likely to bring quantifiable success to the organization. These practices make us more human and, more importantly, better able to see others as human.

The courage of the villagers of Le Chambon was that they saw human beings in need and acted upon that need. They would not describe themselves as particularly brave in reaching out to the Jewish refugees or particularly efficient in meeting their needs, nor would the villagers claim that they saved a large number of lives. They would simply claim they were being Christian. Even in today's world, a Christian can be a very courageous thing to be.

NOTES AND JOURNALING OPPORTUNITIES

I.   Parts of this chapter with which I have mostly agreed in the past:

II. Parts of this chapter with which I have mostly disagreed in the past:

III. Parts of this chapter which have presented new thoughts or information for me:

IV. What's in this chapter . . .

(a) prompts me to remember

(b) prompts me, from years past, to wonder about

(c) prompts me to want to ask, to investigate, to research

(d) prompts me to wonder about changing

(e) prompts me to wonder about the near future in the following ways

(f) prompts me to wonder about the more distant future in the following ways

V. Personal writings, sketches, drawings related to this chapter

Can SOTMOGs Exist outside of Institutional Captivity?

Being Nonsectarian by the Grace of God

> *"A person can think of us in this way: as servants of Christ and stewards of the mysteries of God [SOTMOGs]."*
>
> —1 Corinthians 4:1 (RSV)

Note: This chapter is significantly longer than the others. For that reason, instructors should approach it as two readings or discussions, rather than one.

PART I: INTRODUCING A PAIR OF FOUR-DOLLAR CONCEPTS

Dietrich Bonhoeffer was a Lutheran pastor and teacher. Nazi authorities arrested Bonhoeffer on April 5, 1943, for participating in clandestine conversations and plans that contemplated a future Germany free from Nazi control. In Germany, under the rule of "der Fuhrer" ("the [dictatorial] Leader") Adolf Hitler, such conversations and plans were treasonous and, therefore, had been held secretly in order to protect, as much as possible, the lives of those involved.[1] On July 20, 1944, fifteen and a half months after Bonhoeffer's arrest, a Nazi officer who was secretly opposed to Hitler smuggled a bomb in a briefcase into a military meeting. Placed under a large oaken table, the bomb exploded. A few in the meeting were killed.

Hitler was only slightly injured. He interpreted his survival as a positive sign from God that his leadership and cause would finally prevail against any opposition, whether the opposition was from certain Germans or from the armed forces of the nations engaged against his Third Reich government. World War II continued.[2] On April 9, 1945, with the Allied armies closing on the Nazi command posts, Bonhoeffer, with certain other prisoners, was executed by the Nazi regime.[3]

Okay, so Hitler thought God was on his side. Is there anything else to this, or not? Yes, there is. During the months of his imprisonment prior to his execution, Bonhoeffer wrote and corresponded with others to such an extent that a significant volume of these writings have been compiled and published as *Letters and Papers from Prison*.[4]

Fifteen-plus years after Bonhoeffer's death, and after Hitler's defeat (no matter what he said at the time regarding God's favor), a segment of the Christian community began seriously considering Bonhoeffer's positive use of terms such as "religionless-secular Christians" and "the church in a world-coming-of-age." Religious thinkers and writers John A. T. Robinson, Paul M. Van Buren, William Hamilton, John Godsey, and others focused on either Bonhoeffer's later writings (as from prison) or his earlier writings from the 1920s and 1930s. They appropriated the parts of his writings to which they felt particularly attracted. Each interpreted Bonhoeffer in ways that sought to justify their respective positions,[5] essentially claiming that if Bonhoeffer were alive, he would look favorably on what each of them had written. The "bad news" for all was that Bonhoeffer was not still alive to be advancing his own thoughts. The "good news" was that Bonhoeffer was not going to contradict anyone's interpretation of his writings.

Our intention here is not to offer our own detailed study and analysis of Dietrich Bonhoeffer's theological writings. Neither is our intention to offer a critique of those who have studied Bonhoeffer in depth. Even so, we wonder about some "points" Bonhoeffer raised that seem related to issues that disciples of Jesus face in a dot.com world, even six decades after Bonhoeffer's life was taken.

Some scholars who have studied Bonhoeffer prefer to focus on his earlier writings of theology, which were mildly critical of "institutional" church and culture. Others prefer to focus on his later writings, which are, admittedly, sketchy, less fully developed, and from a time in his life when he felt (rightly so) that the "institutional, traditional" German Christian Church had turned toward the prevailing (Nazi) culture. In the last decade of his life (1935–1945), Bonhoeffer concluded that the "institutional, traditional" church was failing to exemplify forms of discipleship that were consistent with and that encouraged disciples to follow Jesus' way of life. "Church" was failing to hear, discern, and articulate God's word and spirit to the extent that the church's witness of the gospel was not constructively critical of both culture and religion, as Bonhoeffer thought "church" was called to do.

Looking at the ups and downs of historical developments through the six decades since Bonhoeffer's execution and Hitler's defeat and death, one can see that "church" survived, even thrived for a time institutionally, especially in the United States.

Beginning in the late 1950s, through the 1960s, and into the 1970s, the church as an institution in the United States began facing serious challenges related to social changes and upheavals. From the 1980s into the turn of the twenty-first century, the institutional church changed and grew weaker numerically in some forms, and in some cases grew stronger. The numbers of active and affiliated mainline Protestants have declined since the 1960s, while the numbers of independent Christian congregations have increased over the same period of time. Still, though, whether in traditional institutional form or in less formal (less traditionally recognized) institutional form, a Christian religious ethos is quite influential today as a factor in U.S. culture and society.

Adolf Hitler was neither the first person nor the last who applied the "If I survived, God must have been blessing me" rationale to his having personally avoided disaster on a given day.[6] (Look at Luke 13:1–5 for Jesus' response when he was asked about a similar situation.) Surviving, even thriving, at any point in time does not necessarily indicate God's blessing or endorsement. Faltering, even failing and dying, does not necessarily indicate God's anger or disfavor. God's critique is always relevant and timely, as is God's eternal love. In fact, God's love would not be redeeming love without God's critique. Paul wrote to the early church that all persons sin (Rom. 3:23), all persons die, and, in Christ, all will be made alive (1 Cor. 15:22)!

Being disciples of Jesus, then, at least includes and recognizes (1) the abiding nature of God's redeeming (and critiquing) love, (2) the inevitability of death, and (3) the power of God yet to create some form of life-made-new.

Simple Faith?

Two high school students were talking one day. In the course of the conversation, Jamie told Sharee that it was simple to become a Christian. "Here's how simple it is," she said. "To start, pray the 'Sinner's Prayer,' which admits your sin in life to God, asks God's forgiveness, and invites the Lord Jesus to 'come into your heart.' Then you will be saved."

Sharee said, "That's all there is to it?"

"Well, being a disciple is a daily deal, trying to be a follower of Jesus and all that stuff," Jamie said. "But don't worry about that now. It'll come. Just start with the 'Sinner's Prayer.'"

Those like Jamie, who, in their evangelism, teach the "Sinner's Prayer" are very much disciples of Jesus. There's no question about their genuineness as disciples. Sharee's question, though, is important and legitimate. As Jamie responded, discipleship involves more than a one-time prayer, no matter how simple, no matter how complex. Being disciples of Jesus is a daily deal, reaching far into every aspect of life.

We do not argue with the crucial significance of personal repentance and the personal recognition of God's grace in the birth, life, ministry, death by crucifixion, and resurrection of Jesus. We do not argue with the important simplicity of a first prayer in faith or of a beginning statement of faith. We do protest against religious leaders and authorities who imply (1) that the way they teach is the best or the exclusive way to be a disciple of Jesus or (2) that the way of following Jesus has nothing to do with complexity in faith or in life. The current chapter "puts flesh on the bones" of those two protests.

A postmodern ethos and a dot.com world affect our lives. Many persons (perhaps you among them) recognize that in following Jesus faith and discipleship are made possible by God's grace in the midst of life's complexities. This recognition may lead a person to ask how faith and discipleship can be most meaningful when life is as complex as we experience it. Does faith stay "simple" and create "good feelings" every time possible? Theoretically, against long odds, faith in life might work out that way, but the odds are much more weighted toward faith being "put to work" through mistakes, tragedy, and difficult choices.

Hollywood Endings: So Very Rare

In 1952, Bernard Malamud wrote a baseball novel titled *The Natural*.[7] In 1984, Tri-Star Pictures lit up the big screen with *The Natural* as a "Hollywood movie," although with a significantly different twist at the end.[8] While altering one part or another of a book to create a movie's screenplay is not unusual, *The Natural*'s Hollywood ending is notably different from the novel. Malamud was still alive at the time, and he no doubt gave the movie's producer a green light on the changed ending. In both the novel and the movie, the primary character, Roy Hobbs, takes a bribe to "throw" or give a subpar performance in the game that will determine the league championship. In both the novel and the movie, Roy decides against throwing the game. In the movie, he returns the money to those who bribed him before the game, telling them that he plans to give the best performance his physically injured self can give. In the novel, Roy only decides with certainty to give his best during the playing of the game itself.

In the movie, Hobbs, even with his strength compromised by the flare-up of a reopened surgical wound, still manages to smash a game-winning home run, trumping his opponents, and refuting any bribery rumors that may have been leaked to the press. In the novel, however, the "original" Roy Hobbs, in the final inning, strikes out. The game is lost. Roy departs the field and clubhouse immediately and returns the money, in the process physically punching out those who had bribed him. The next morning, the local newspaper reports with headlines the embarrassing rumor that Roy "had taken a bribe."[9]

In the novel, Roy, in the end, acts with the same repentance and turn to integrity that are portrayed in the movie. Given his last-inning strikeout in the original story, he could not prove that he had not kept the money and thrown the game. Roy can live with knowing he did his best to counter his own unethical and illegal action, but still he is publicly shamed. There's no avoiding that disgrace, because the bribe offering power brokers who were paid back their money surely aren't speaking up to defend Roy's honor.

The ending of Malamud's novel comes closer to the way real life usually is. Most often, we do not find ourselves in situations where we have an opportunity to overcome a personal failing with a self-engineered public victory. Fewer still are the occasions in which we succeed when the opportunity materializes. When it's most clear to us that life is messy and complex, even when guilt and shame become public, what does a person do who has desired only simplicity in faith and a "clean, great feeling" about faith? Such faith now seems oversimplified and absolutely inadequate.

This chapter invites readers to prepare to undertake a "canyon" journey if they (you!) have ever wondered about the potential problem of "faith oversimplified," and if they (you!) have ever yearned for potentially meaningful alternatives. We inquire about ways and look for "handles" by which faith and discipleship following Jesus—equal to the challenge of life's complexities—can be practiced daily and faithfully. We explore some of the less frequently examined and diverse ways—negative and positive (positively eccentric!)—in which disciples of Jesus have practiced faith differently across the ages. We're convinced no one can be hurt as we offer an orientation for your imaginary canyon journey, and if anyone benefits from this orientation, that's great!

THE GRAND CANYON

If you take a trip to the Grand Canyon, you have several options when considering the ways to see it. You may stand up top and view with your own eyes. You may enhance your vision with binoculars or a telescope. You may take a helicopter or airplane ride over the canyon. You may ride on the back of a mule down a trail into the canyon, or you may hike into the canyon on your own power. Even if one rides a mule or hikes on one's own two feet or goes in one's wheelchair, some persons are more interested in general panoramic views; others are more interested in the finest details, including the smallest fossils and the rock formation layer changes in the canyon walls.

Being disciples of Jesus is, we think, an endeavor best undertaken when "hikers" are prepared with some informational tools for analyzing: (1) what will be observed on the way; and (2) what challenges and adversity might arise. For example, let's imagine hiking in the summer, at sunset, along the river in the bottom of the canyon. Small frogs are seen hopping off into the grass as you make your way along the trail. One person might say, "Isn't it neat to see the little frogs at sunset?" Another person might say, "Little frogs make a tasty meal for rattlesnakes, copperheads, and water moccasins. Does anyone know if those types of poisonous snakes are native to the area of the Grand Canyon? If so, the presence of little frogs should serve as a signal to us to watch, as we hike, for poisonous snakes lying in wait for a supper of little frogs." Hiking humans, turning a corner in the trail and surprising a poisonous snake, can receive the same treatment that the snake intends for the hopping frogs.

Hopping frogs may be cute. To the prepared hiker, beyond their cuteness, they are a sign for caution, not because they themselves pose any danger, but because of the fundamentals of the canyon's ecosystem, about which we can ill afford to be underinformed or unaware. Let's prepare ourselves with an adequate orientation.

Keep It Simple?

We assume that if you have read this far, you either have been or are becoming interested in at least some of the finer details of being disciples of Jesus. As has been both stated and implied, not every person feels this way. Rather frequently, persons in roles of religious authority, or pretending to be in roles of authority, say to listeners that their faith needs to take shape according to the prescribed pattern of the authority person: "Because I said so. . . ."

If involved in a conversation with the two of us as we write this book, the "authority figure" Christians might say to us: "If you tell people that the Christian faith is complex, they'll stay away. Keep it simple in the communication, because that's the way 'they' want it. Anything complex will confuse them." That statement might be true for many persons, and, if it's fine with those persons, that's fine with us.

We in fact agree that certain important basics ("God is love," "Jesus is Lord," etc.) can be understood as foundational and simple. We are equally convinced, however, that many "would-be" or "once were" disciples of Jesus no longer consider themselves parts of faith communities because churches have failed to offer serious alternatives to the "keep it simple" perspective. Some people may have already departed certain communities of faith because faith "became too complex." Other people may also have already departed because the community of faith did not engagingly invite them to explore complexities in the intersections of life and faith! Included among the already departed or those contemplating departure are folks who say, "It appears to me that church folk much of the time either ignore or cover up inconsistencies, hypocrisies, and discrepancies between what Jesus taught and what churches and church officers sometimes do. They mostly either hide their problematic issues, or they act as if they are in denial about them."

"Keep it simple" advocates of Christianity often ignore or would like to keep secret two important considerations, especially if one takes seriously the fact that we cannot escape the postmodern, dot.com world in which we live. Are you ready for this pair of four-dollar words? "Hermeneutics" is one. "Ecclesiology" is the other.

Hermeneutics is the science of interpretive methods, how something is interpreted. In this case, one "something" is how a person or group interprets the Bible as Scripture.[10] The other "something" is how a person or group interprets "church" and "church as an extended faith community of God's people." Hermeneutics, then, also can "inform" or influence how one understands or what one believes related to the "church" or "extended community of faith."

The hermeneutic of the biblical inerrantist is based on an understanding that the Bible is basically a direct printout of God's dictation. If you have an "inerrant hermeneutic," you are convinced that the Bible as Scripture is free of any serious inaccuracies. All angles of truth are timelessly applicable without qualification. Dispute with the text of Scripture is less permissible than is a dispute with God personally through prayer.

An inerrant hermeneutic could be at odds with an "anthology hermeneutic," which views each book of the Bible as being a product of a particular context or set of circumstances. The messages about God or about God's people, for example, from the various books written from various time periods and places might vary so much that teachings surface that conflict with one another.

One example of such a direct conflict is how Nehemiah 13:23–27 forbids the marriage of pure blood-line Israelite men to Moabite women. This stance directly conflicts with God's blessing on the marriage of Boaz (an Israelite) to Ruth (from Moab) narrated in Ruth 4:13–22. Isn't it all the more scandalous to Nehemiah that Boaz and Ruth's son, Obed, becomes the grandfather of King David (!) and a direct ancestor of Mary's husband, Joseph, head of the household of Jesus (Matt. 1:5)?!

Such variations and conflicts vex the person or group from the "inerrant hermeneutic school" more than the person from an "anthology hermeneutic school." The inerrantist faces the challenge of explaining competing perspectives regarding God and God's people as expressed in Scripture. The "anthologist," in contrast, has no inherent need to resolve conflicting teachings from book to book in the Bible, or within a given book, because the anthologist's hermeneutic does not "stand or fall" on smoothing out or resolving existing inconsistencies or apparent contradictions.

Ecclesiology is a cousin of hermeneutics. Not many "keep it simple" advocates of Christianity will tell you that either. While ecclesiology is the study of (1) the organizational connections and relationships of faith communities ("churches") and (2) why and how they structure themselves and function in the ways they do, a primary influence in the formation of many church structures and the authority of those structures has roots in the books of the Bible, from different interpretations, as you might guess.

The ecclesiology of the pope in Rome differs from the ecclesiology of the pastor of the Baptist church in suburban Charlotte, North Carolina. Both the pope and the Baptist pastor will have an ecclesiology different from the Fellowship of the Holy Ghost Church on a corner in Houston, Texas. Traditional categories of denominational structures are basically three in number: (a) episcopal-type church structures, which include bishops exercising significant governing authority; (b) presbyterian-type church structures, which rely on elders who are elected by congregations to govern the ministry efforts of churches; and (c) congregational-type churches, which govern themselves (locally), with associations and alliances with other congregations being voluntary (rather than obligatory, as with episcopal and presbyterian forms).

Do hermeneutics and ecclesiology sound boring? Give us a chance to convince you that you already make (or accept others') judgments and hold opinions about hermeneutics and ecclesiology, whether you realize it or not. What if someone says, "I believe the Bible expresses God's truth for all times and does so without error" or, "I only accept as God's true word those parts of the Bible that seem to advocate God's love for everyone"? What if someone says, "I rely totally on what this or that church leader or church group says" or, "I never believe what church leaders or church councils say unless I agree with them"? The first two of these statements express two types of hermeneutics and the second express two types of ecclesiologies. In between the statements of each of those two pairs are more perspectives than the world has types of butterflies.

Give us a chance to convince you also that hermeneutics and ecclesiology may be anything but boring. Many persons in a dot.com world and postmodern ethos might say, "The church, or communities of faith, have nothing relevant to offer me." Others might say, "The church is owned by the cultures in which it's set. Why bother?" Those opinions can be expressed and believed. Yet what if some or many who spoke so critically of the institutional church were still genuinely interested in faith as lived and revealed in Jesus? And what if churches continue to discredit, downplay, and ignore such critiques as less important than the priority of keeping current members convinced of their own rightness, and thereby keeping them satisfied?

We are nevertheless convinced that, with the biblical traditions honestly hand-in-hand with science, history, and the arts, avenues or trails do lead away from irrelevance and boredom and, rather, lead in the direction of faith-excitement and challenges that persons may never before have experienced. As you journey through the Great Canyon of discipleship, we hope that an honest intersecting of Scripture, hermeneutics, ecclesiology, science, history, and the arts will enliven and strengthen your life and faith, and the lives and faith of others. With that goal, let's examine a few elements and clues from a few hermeneutical and ecclesiological "systems." Let's see how they vary. Let's see what wisdom can be gleaned for each person who desires to grow out of confusion and into a maturing (but not stuffy!!) faithfulness as a disciple of Jesus in this dot.com world.

Various Interpretations

Imagine a conversation between two persons of any age, gender, time period, or place. One says, "What you say your group believes has me thinking that your group really isn't part of the true believing community in our faith tradition the way my group is." The second responds, "We are too!" The first says, "You are not!" The second, "Are too!" The first, "Are not!" and on and on, until the second responds with an equal accusation: "I think your group is the one not part of the true believing community in this faith tradition the way my group is." To which the first responds, "Yes, we are!" The second says, "No, you're not!" then "Are too!" and "Are not!" all over again.[11]

Conversations about who, or whose group, is part of "the true believing community" in a particular faith tradition might sound like a meaningless and irrelevant argument to many persons who are part of the postmodern ethos and dot.com world. "Who cares?" they might say. Somebody must care. History records that words of disagreement have been shouted, penned, and printed. Blood has been spilled. Innumerable groups (Christians and others) have competed, and still today are competing, for the superiority, purity, and sometimes the survival of their respective religious convictions.

As recipients of faith-and-belief traditions and ways of thinking that are centuries old, people who sense a call to be disciples of Jesus in the twenty-first century also ask, at least from time to time: "Who's in?" "Who's out?" "Who's 'true to the faith'?" "Who's hypocritical, heretical, or apostate?" One person or group may feel such questions are mandatory and essential. Another person or group may feel such questions are unimportant and distracting. We are convinced that trails wind through the canyon between "mandatory and essential" and "unimportant and distracting." This chapter presumes that traveling those trails is a major element of being disciples of Jesus in a dot.com world.

We further presume that the ones traveling those trails no more resemble people who were Jesus' disciples in the first century than every aspect of our modes of travel or agronomy are identical to those in the first century where and when Jesus lived. In other words, the Bible does not give absolute guidance about the particulars of every issue in the twenty-first (or any other) century. That's because its writings are neither nonhistorical, ahistorical, nor are they transhistorical writings.

First, the Bible stories and teachings happen within history; therefore, they are historical rather than being nonhistorical or ahistorical. Don't take this claim to mean that the Bible is primarily a book objectively citing historical events or developments. To the contrary, most parts of the Bible never exemplify anything approaching objective history, while every part of the Bible has roots in history and in various historical contexts (times, places, situations, cultures). Moreover, history and contextual values are primary components to consider when moving through any present-day canyons of judgments, determinations, and opinions.

Second, Bible stories and teachings cannot be labeled as uniformly transhistorical. Transhistorical means "across history" much like a roof spans a covered stadium below. Certain time periods and geographic areas have always lain beyond the umbrella of what's covered in Scripture. Such time periods and geographic areas are not, however, beyond the umbrella of God's presence. That's why we say God's word and spirit testify through Scripture into every time and place. That's also why we say, "Interpretive work is required."

We are convinced that God is somehow mysteriously in the midst of Scripture and of deliberations, debates, disagreements, and decisions about diverse interpretations and diverse applications that are part of human life. We also believe that we often cannot easily discern how God exactly is present in a given time and place. God can certainly face danger and evil in historical, real-life situations, and God can be in situations safe and pleasant. Either way God is "out on the grounds," however accurate it might also be to say that God is invincible, "above," or "up there."

Are You Willing to Be Damned?

A story has been retold among the variety of Presbyterian-type church traditions. The story comes from the first half of the 1900s, possibly from Scotland or from the southern, northeastern, or Ohio River areas of the United States. The regional gathering was examining candidates who had completed their formal college and theological graduate school (seminary) requirements. The examination consisted of spontaneous verbal questions from various ministers and member elders of the region's several churches to the candidate for ordination to the ministry of Word and Sacrament. The exam had been tough and long. At last, an elder rose to pose an often-asked "insider" question. The question is related to the church's roots among the teachings of John Calvin and those, decades later, who thought themselves related to Calvin in their own particular interpretations. The elder said, "My question is, 'Are you willing to be damned, if your being damned would bring glory to God?'"

The weary yet still resolute and undaunted candidate never wavered. "Sir," he said, "I am, and more: I'm willing for this entire presbytery to be damned if it would bring glory to God." As the story goes, the often-austere elders and ministers in attendance erupted with laughter, cheers, and applause, voting overwhelmingly to approve the candidate for ordination.

That traditional question of "classical" Presbyterian types sounds especially odd to many Christians and others (even to many "modern/postmodern/dot.com" Presbyterians!) in a postmodern ethos and dot.com world. First, who wants to be damned—ever? Second, how can any sensible understanding of God imply that God wants anyone to be damned in order to further God's purposes? Third, doesn't that sound too close to "suicide bombing" in the name of one's religious cause for anyone even to mention it aloud?

The Calvinist "litmus-test question" is of course hypothetical and hyperbolic. It does not ask about a real situation, and it exaggerates in the way it asks the question itself. Regarding the third question in the previous paragraph and a reflex critique of the Calvinists' inside interrogative, the exam query does sound uncomfortably close to something like, "Would you be willing to give your life for the cause of God?" which we hear that radical, fundamentalist Muslims and others ask their followers. Even though, sadly, Christians at times through the ages have persecuted, maimed, and killed for God in the name of Jesus, neither such a meaning nor such a response is at all what's at the heart of the Calvinists' traditional question.

Far closer to the point is, in fact, what Muslim brothers and sisters intend with the general definition of the word *jihad*,[12] which tends to mean "holy quest" or "quest in the service of the One who is holy." Discipleship in the way and spirit of Jesus in every day and time is exactly that: a quest in the service of the One who is holy. Included in that quest, if undertaken with one's entire being and self, is a willingness to give up everything, if giving up everything would bring glory and honor to God! Even the hyperbolic nature of the question yet challenges us to be diligent in serving God daily as radically faithful stewards of all the gifts we are given. (Remember from chapter 5: "Everything is stewardship!") Such a view (1) of the gifts God gives; (2) of the salvation, wholeness, and healing that God bestows; and (3) of the stewardship God desires and expects can certainly create hesitation. Remember how Jesus personally faced the hesitation of those whom he called and invited to the journey of discipleship (Luke 9:57–62, and elsewhere)?

Twenty-five to thirty years after Jesus, the apostle Paul was confronted with questions about "Who is 'really' in God's 'true' group?" which included the implication that he might not really be in God's true group. He answered his critics, writing, "Think of us in this way, as servants of Christ and stewards of God's mysteries" (1 Cor. 4:1). "Stewards of God's mysteries" is the translation of the New Revised Standard Version. The "old" Revised Standard Version translated the same Greek words slightly differently: "stewards of the mysteries of God." The RSV translation, if one appropriates the first letter of each word, enables us to speak of God calling every person to be a "SOTMOG."

As the question, "Are you willing to be damned, if your being damned would bring glory to God?" raises questions about its meanings, being "stewards of the mysteries of God" also has raised questions since Paul first penned the phrase.

• Some people have proposed and advanced arguments that these mysteries were "special and particular secrets" of the faith.
• Some people have said that these mysteries are the sacraments of the church over which the clergy are appointed stewards (exclusively).
• Some people have understood these mysteries to be the "stumbling block" (also translated "scandal") of Jesus' life, ministry, death, resurrection, and continuing redeeming presence through the Spirit of God. Paul employs this characterization in 1 Corinthians 1:23.[13]

In other words, that God would become human is beyond routine human notions. Maybe it's not beyond fantasy, but it is beyond routine (even religious) human notions that understand God as being distinct or separate from human beings. God, in God's distinctiveness or separateness, would presumably be defiled and disgraced by commingling with us humans. (One can stumble over a God who shows up among us with such outrageous, boundary-crossing relatedness!)

This third understanding of God's mysteries offers the widest and deepest possibilities for disciples of Jesus in a postmodern ethos and dot.com world, and how such an understanding can "stir things up"! If we can legitimately conclude—or at least explore—that all disciples of Jesus are "stewards of the mysteries of God" (SOTMOGs!), then immense implications exist for our (1) "being church in history and world," (2) "being interpreters of Scripture," and (3) "being human in creation."

PART II: PREPARING FOR THE HIKE

Out in the Great (discipleship) Canyon, not everyone has seen (in the past), sees now (in the present), or will see (in the future) the same need for applying biblical values and teachings that you do. Also, disagreements even take place between people who agree that biblical values and teachings are important on which biblical values and teachings apply. Interpretations differ across the board.

European settlers began arriving on the island of Tasmania in the early 1800s. On Tasmania, they found many of the same types of wildlife that had been encountered in Australia. One animal on the island was rather different from others observed in Australia, canine enough in appearance for many to name it the "Tasmanian wolf." The animal also had a series of dark stripes descending down its sides from across the top of its back. For this reason, some people called it the "Tasmanian tiger." Equally unusual to many observers, the creature was a marsupial, with the pouch facing "backward" on the underside of the female (similar to the wolverine-like "Tasmanian devil"), and its tail was more kangaroo-like than canine- or feline-like. The animal's scientific name, in shortened form, is simply "thylacine."

The settlers with European backgrounds introduced sheep to Tasmania in the 1820s and 1830s. After a short period of time, they became convinced that the carnivorous (and relatively slow afoot) thylacine were finding the sheep easier prey than wallabies, etc. In 1888, the government placed a bounty on the shy animal. In 1910, a distemper-like epidemic probably killed many of the thylacine that had escaped the bounty hunters. The last one in captivity died in the mid-1930s; at the same time, the government belatedly passed a law protecting the species from all hunting. Periodically, since 1936, sightings or evidence of thylacine surface from sparsely settled parts of Tasmania, yet these claims have done more to keep hope alive than to provide evidence that thylacine actually continue to exist today.[14]

Tasmania's national coat of arms, approved in 1917 by the reigning monarch of the British Empire, King George V, when the thylacine were becoming rarer and rarer, offers a continual and ironic reminder of Tasmania's stewardship of the thylacine. The shield of the coat of arms is supported on the right and the left by a thylacine, each facing the other. The motto on the scroll beneath is "*Ubertas et Fidelitas,*" Latin for "abundance and faithfulness."[15] The presence of the two thylacine on the coat of arms reminds every person who knows the story how aspects of life of which a person or group is most proud (the abundance of a country and the faithfulness of the nation's citizens) ironically can be overlooked, neglected, or abused.

The cross of Jesus is like that. God's people can be very proud of God's love known through God's covenant with the larger family of Abraham; through God's liberating of Hebrew slaves in Egypt; and through the life, ministry, death, and resurrection of Jesus. At the same time, while revering and honoring the cross, Christians—along with others of God's people in their own ways—decade after decade, week after week, can overlook, neglect, and abuse fellow citizens in this world and aspects of the global ecosystem. The biblical tradition calls that "sin," even when we are adoring the cross at the same time.

The existence of the remainder of God's creation does not depend on the existence of the thylacine. Can we, though, learn from this bit of

Tasmanian history? Anytime a larger community of God's people is preoccupied with their own needs, desires, and goals (even protecting livestock), the odds increase that they will not easily see an unfortunate possibility growing into a probability. What we do not recognize, we do not research and address for remedy, even when a remedy is crucial.

Some disciples of Jesus say that Jesus' death on the cross is the remedy for sin. However true that is, Jesus' death on the cross is no excuse for disciples of Jesus pretending that sin in some of its forms can be selectively emphasized and in other forms just as selectively underemphasized, even disregarded.

To paraphrase the title of a once-upon-a-time television comedy, *Men Behaving Badly,* our contention is that "Church Behaving Badly" is no situation comedy, but is an often underresearched, undertold, and underremembered story. We have more skeletons in the closets of the Church than a grade-B horror movie. Inquisitions, executions, crusades, shunnings, exclusions, etc., are part of our history across the centuries in almost every part of the world. Many people who desire to be disciples of Jesus and many people who claim to be disciples in a consumer-and-pleasure world are quite comfortable not discussing or ever learning much about "Church Behaving Badly."

While this short book cannot detail the lows of faithfulness and highs of hypocrisy through the centuries of God's people worshiping and serving as various faith communities, we can point to a few select examples. We also can offer guidance in reading the Bible (hermeneutics) and "being church" (ecclesiology) that may be helpful in our ongoing journey as disciples of Jesus through the Great Canyon of life and history.

As your canyon guides, let us say that in our own journeys through the Great Canyon we've been helped when employing an "east of Eden hermeneutic" (eoEh) and a "stewards of the mysteries of God ecclesiology" (sotmoGe). "Wait a minute," you may say. "You didn't mention an 'east of Eden hermeneutic' or a 'stewards of the mysteries of God ecclesiology' in the earlier examples." Right. We didn't. We have also not mentioned many others that a person or group might appropriate and use. We simply recommend these two, given the way and ways life is in the dot.com world where we seek to be Jesus' faithful disciples. We can discuss these two now before you depart on the trail through the Great Canyon.

"East of Eden" Everywhere We Go

Genesis 3:1–7 conveys a story of human beings attempting to "have life their way" (remember the Burger King commercial?). They also attempt to maneuver themselves into a place where, because they hope that they will be so satisfied, the rest of the world might say to them, "We love to see you smile" (remember the McDonald's commercial?). In any sense of what is holy, this outcome simply cannot be the result, not short-term, not long-term, not so long as the Lord of heaven and earth is Lord. At the conclusion of this episode in Genesis, the owner of the garden called Eden evicts the overreaching human stewards with the result that they live the days of their lives beyond the east gate of Eden. The owner locks the gate behind them—forever.

An "east of Eden" hermeneutic (eoEh) sees this story as a model by which much of life and Scripture can be understood. Seven generalized "working conclusions" can be deduced from reading Genesis to Revelation with an eoE hermeneutic.

1. It's a flawed world, with much of the "flawedness" resulting from human (our) "overreaching"—attempting to live beyond what's healthy—and human (our) underreaching—failing to live up to the level of health and responsibility that God desires and intends.
2. We're all flawed as human beings.
3. We need not obsess over desires for or expectations of perfection or perfect consistency. Perfection is not going to happen.
4. God is in the midst of God's people and God's world, and present more often with vulnerable love, justice, and mercy, than with overriding power, as we understand overriding power.
5. God is not limited by creation or creatures (including us).
6. Neither is God defiled by being among creation or among God's people, even when present (and hurt, even killed!) in the vulnerability of love.
7. God calls us and manifests God's self in the world to the end that God's people can daily live and grow differently from whom we would shape ourselves to be, either in simply surviving or in cunningly attempting to exalt ourselves. By God's ever present grace (eccentric in judgment and in mercy!), God mysteriously accomplishes bit by bit and day by day what God desires to accomplish. God's desired accomplishments include redeeming and making new the lives of God's people in creation.

The east of Eden hermeneutic, though, becomes most helpful when envisioning what human beings do when we realize that the gate is shut and locked behind us, and the key is locked back on the inside (if God hasn't thrown away the key altogether!). Just as when we lock keys inside our cars, houses, apartments, storerooms, or offices, or when we lose or forget the access number or password to the security system, a degree of panic and frustration arises. Even so, from Genesis 4 through Revelation 22, the biblical story continues beyond the "clanging shut of the gate, locked forever."

To our way of thinking, the Bible (viewed through the lenses of our east of Eden hermeneutic) describes, in different ways, how dissatisfied human beings try continually to figure out ways to break into Eden or deceptively to re-create Eden. Is it amusing, or sad, to imagine human beings trekking to the backside of the fence around Eden and finding a place to climb over, or orchestrating a scheme to dig under, in order to get back inside? Or deciding that although we find ourselves east of Eden, we should now build or create for God a new version of Eden out here where we are?

Our human yearning for perfection and purity—for life experiences, relationships, and even institutions without flaws, failure, pain, loss, grief, etc.—can be understood from the symbolism and metaphorical accuracy of this Genesis story. Furthermore, the Holiness Code tradition, a primary example of which is described in the book of Leviticus, furthers this perspective. Leviticus 11:44, 19:2, and 20:26 record the word of the Lord to Moses: "You shall be holy, for I the Lord your God am holy."

"Holiness," "purity," and "perfection" are three cousins. They are very much biblical subjects. The Holiness codes, developed particularly in the tradition of those who wrote Leviticus, are presented as words from God. These teachings indicate the crucial importance of pleasing God with a strict following of covenant obligations. The writers of Leviticus, in their time period, "heard" God placing "a different spin" on God's teachings from Exodus, Deuteronomy, and related writings. Still, the covenant obligations of Leviticus included the practice of justice for persons known and unknown, plus guidelines for "holiness" in personal habits and worship practices.[16]

These words and teachings have a legacy and influence of immense proportions. Much of the intent of the "holiness and purity codes" is undoubtedly theological, with a goal of God's people clearly identifying themselves as unique and distinct, "different from" the cultures of non-Israelites where they found themselves.

This part of the Judeo-Christian faith tradition influences many followers of Jesus to say, "If you/we don't strive for such holiness, you/we will eliminate any possibility of perfection with purity for our lives as disciples. We'll then be guilty of underachieving as God's stewards of the world, of life, and of faith." People who raise that critique believe God wants and expects us to be persons who strive for building God's kingdom on earth. They believe that God gives grace so that we can and will be at work building God's kingdom and that any failure to apply ourselves with that goal in mind is "sin."

You can probably see that a serious "fork-in-the-trail" difference in interpretation exists between those who adopt something like our east of Eden hermeneutic and others who prefer a Holiness (Purity) Code basis for discipleship or a "building and reinforcing God's kingdom for perfection with purity" hermeneutic.

We do not believe that God endorses underachieving. We do believe, though, that innumerable efforts to "fulfill every aspect of the Holiness (Purity) Code" and to "build and reinforce God's kingdom for perfection and purity" appear every so often in two forms: (1) Persons attempt to climb the fence of the garden from which we humans have long been banished; or (2) persons attempt to build walls and fences for separating themselves (ourselves) from others "out there" east of Eden.

The Bible indeed records that Jesus used the phrase, "Be perfect, therefore, as your heavenly Father is perfect" (Matt. 5:48). We noted, in chapter 4, that the word frequently translated to English as "perfect" can also be translated "be made whole" or "be made complete." This alternate translation could indicate a process of turning toward God's ways as God's spirit leads, yet without expecting God to give us "perfection" or "purity" as we would define those categories (or as we would reshape other persons and the world according to such categories).

The elements of the Holiness Code relating to personal habits, as with the dietary rules and sexuality laws, became criteria for deciding "cleanliness" and uncleanliness, purity and impurity, and for judging who was faithful to God and who was not. Remember also, though, within the Bible, that the story of Ruth very likely was told and written as a dissent against Holiness Code advocates who claimed God would not bless marriages to non-Israelites, of whom Ruth was one. Boaz and Ruth were not the "poster couple" of the strict Holiness Code advocates!

In the case of both the theological and the practical, Jesus—Jewish though he was (and related to Boaz and Ruth [!], at least sort of)—time and again "bent the rules" and offered his own interpretation of those codes. He would do that if he perceived that following the code strictly would "work against" the authentic human needs of "regular human beings" (for example, Mark 1:41 and Mark 2:23–28).

In the earliest decades of the Church (after Jesus' crucifixion), key debates evolved over matters related to "holiness and purity" requirements and non-Jewish folk. The key debates on both "distinct and unique" and "dietary" aspects of the Holiness Codes from the Jewish tradition were judged (following what were understood to be revelations from God) to be optional for disciples of Jesus (Acts 10:1–11:18). In related teachings, disciples of Jesus were encouraged to be respectful of others who observed religious traditions and practices differently, often with a sense of obligation. Such obligatiory practices by certain groups were rooted in their own interpretations of Scripture and tradition, leading them to disagree with those who thought the same practices were optional, specifically eating meat previously dedicated to idols (1 Cor. 8:1–13). A similar tolerance was considered important when "schools" of disciples of Jesus became aware (often painfully aware) of differing interpretations among themselves regarding Scripture, specifically about circumcision (Gal. 2:1–4:20; 5:2–15).

We may further wonder—legitimately—where God is in this "east of Eden" interpretative method. We cannot say with certainty, yet we may discover a major clue in the original Eden story wherein God decides to take a stroll in the garden called Eden. In the process, God checks on the humans there and discovers that they are hiding, with the cause being sin and guilt (Genesis 3:8–13). If God once strolled in the garden and desired a working fellowship and healthy relationship with human beings, evidence in the Bible indicates God may well still be strolling among the humans (and all the rest) of creation.

What if God is not even back inside Eden anymore, having given up on Eden and deciding the world as we now experience the world will be God's "theater of operation" for the long-term present? How much more ludicrous could all human efforts to break back into Eden appear? Or how much more pitiable could our efforts be to reconstruct Eden out in the world as we now experience the world, all the while building and reinforcing with the (obsessive?!) goal of holiness, perfection, and purity, as we define and seek to experience perfection and purity? (Might Jesus have been thinking something like this in those instances when he skirted, reinterpreted, and downplayed "purity obligations" and "perfection expectations" as he did?)

The "holiness tradition" is very much a part of the Judeo-Christian tradition, and similar guidelines exist for Muslims. Some people, however, find that a strict adherence to many details of the Holiness Code goes beyond what they think God is willing to accept. The unhelpful "baggage" of holiness and purity obligations and of perfection expectations almost invariably sends one down a trail or trails that unrealistically raise expectations of God and of life in any culture or time period. An east of Eden hermeneutic, rather, anticipates a genuineness and authenticity in our being human that accepts and acknowledges our "flawedness," our vulnerability, and our living "east of Eden" as we do.

"Made in the image of God" implies a genuineness and authenticity of this sort when Jesus is the model of God's image (born in poverty, growing, learning, teaching, healing, arrested, killed, and resurrected by God's mysterious power for life-made-new). This Jesus is then the model whom disciples of Jesus understand themselves called to follow in the journey through the Great Canyon, which is very much east of Eden.

Both the hermeneutics stuff and the ecclesiology stuff are essential for evaluating what and whom you will encounter on your journey through the Great Canyon. From the canyon floor all the way to the rim, the fossil record, the geologic formations, the flora and the fauna, the other persons you encounter, and your own thoughts, words, and actions can be evaluated in useful and healthy ways. This journey is increasingly possible for people who develop broadening interpretive skills with regard to (1) what people have thought, said, and done through history; (2) the content and contexts of the Bible; (3) scientific method; and (4) cultural needs and desires.

IDOLATRY AND TYRANNY

Many have said that sin often takes the form of idolatry or tyranny, or both.[17] Idolatry amounts to accepting and maintaining as a priority ("worshiping") that which is more counterfeit than genuine and authentic. To apply the "Burger King" slogan mentioned previously, idolatry can be present when we say, "I will have this my way, thank you," regardless of what the Lord's word and spirit might be seeking differently. Idolatry can be a reality daily in the classifications of both what is "sacred" and what is secular, what seems religious and what seems nonreligious.

Tyranny is what people do when we exercise manipulative or forceful control of a situation according to what we want. We do that because we think that what we want is the way this "deal" ought to be. Some have characterized both tyranny and idolatry as "the human wanting and attempting to be God." ("I'll have it my way, thank you.")

Tyranny has at least two forms. One is more obvious and overt. The obvious form of tyranny is that of one exerting power over another, or of many exerting power over many others. We easily see how this form of tyranny is directly related to idolatry: "I'll have you be my way."

Another form of tyranny is less obvious—more subtle and manipulative—than overtly forceful. It's a relationship characterized by coercive persuasion, the key word being "coercive." This type of tyranny sends the message, "We love to see you smile; and you'll be smiling when you do what I/we suggest (or demand)." It also carries an unspoken message, "You will be in pain if you don't do what I/we suggest (or demand)." This type of tyranny can be exercised by a dictatorial government demanding conformity from citizens who are oppressed and are denied freedom by that dictatorial government. Church institutions, in their own ways and in various times and places, have been known to act similarly, with the result that diversity and processes for dissent are stifled. An abusive family member can also tyrannize another family member, as a worker can tyrannize associates.

The subtle form of tyranny which communicates that it "loves to see you smile" is the tyranny that a culture, a business, a religious community, or a person can assert. It seeks the voluntary, "codependent" involvement of another person or group, with persuasion like, "Believe me: You need this or that in this relationship, and you will be pleased when you get what we offer in exchange for your money, loyalty, conformity, etc."

This subtle form of tyranny dangles the promise and pleasure of personal satisfaction as a reward for cooperation or submission. Religious communities, sororities, fraternities, political parties, and other groups confer the benefits of membership in exchange for (1) "dues," (2) adherence to agreed-upon rules, and (3) commonly held beliefs, traditions, etc.

Are groups always either overtly or subtly tyrannical? No.

If you get pleasure in return for your dues, as in swimming at a swim club, membership can be positive and healthy. If you receive a meaningful sense of belonging to a larger community of faith when contributing time, energy, money, and love as part of a religious group, such membership is positive and healthy.

Are all rules and laws stifling or exploitational with the result that human freedom is denied? No.

John Calvin was a sixteenth-century Frenchman who lived much of his adult life in Switzerland. More than once, Calvin referred to contrasting images of "the abyss" and "the labyrinth."[18] In Calvin's understanding, the abyss is the chaos of everyone's unbridled, unchecked freedom. It's anarchy. The labyrinth is the weaving of rules and regulations to such an extent that freedom within constructive boundaries is potentially cramped or threatened.

Any culture (religious, state, ethnic, etc.) has the potential, intentionally or unintentionally, to manifest and promote the abyss at certain times and the labyrinth at other times.

In chapter 3, we noted our preference for "faithful eccentricity" as a variation on the perhaps more frequently understood notion of Jesus' disciples being countercultural. Building on the themes introduced in chapters 3 and 4 (God's grace as "great gift"), let's look further at (1) how faithful eccentricity characterizes the discipleship of Jesus' followers and (2) how such faithful eccentricity is made possible in given contexts by God's grace. We explore further here our SOTMOG ecclesiology.

We believe living in a dot.com world and postmodern ethos creates options and opportunities. One key question, derived largely from examining Scripture and history, is, "How might the church be nonsectarian in addition to faithfully eccentric?" As part of a "living tradition" of faith, we feel a sense of responsibility both to God and to the larger community of faith to which we are related—historical, ecumenical, and geographic as that "larger community of faith" is.

Seeing the church as nonsectarian involves, first, considering ways in which the church or religious communities generally make decisions to be sectarian. The word "sect," from the past participle form of the Latin word *sequor,* means "to follow" as in following a pathway, a course of conduct, or school of thought. Moreover, if you use the four letters "s-e-c-t" as they are part of a word like "intersect," the Latin word of origin is the past participle form of the word *secare (sectus),* which means "to cut."19

To be sectarian, then ("any way you cut it"!) from the Latin means to pursue a certain path. One can think of this word as clearing a path or cutting a line of brush to build a fence. Either way, "sect" means one is moving along a path, which, in itself, is generally understood as being more narrow than broad.

In a more specific sense, when a group claims to be, or is labeled as being, a sect, we tend to think that the group has chosen a narrow way to go and be, which they prefer to adopting a broader perspective. The fear usually is that to adopt a broader perspective or view of life is to risk the dreaded acculturation that the particular group seeks to avoid. If the group becomes too acculturated, they fear they will lose their distinctiveness. Sects almost always view the broader culture as posing a major threat, whether the culture pretends to pose no threat or whether the culture is overtly hostile.

Religious groups, whether large or small, can and frequently do adopt a sectarian perspective, cutting a path of withdrawal to a significant extent from society/culture generally. They clear a path to build a fenceline between themselves and society/culture. Jesus' disciples have two immensely important questions to ponder:

1. *Is every fenceline or boundary that distinguishes one group or tradition from others necessarily "bad" or necessarily sacred as a fence or boundary in and of itself?* No; but to avoid becoming captive to one's own

institutional, clannish, purity, holiness, or perfection tendencies, each group or tradition does well to enable itself to "breathe." This exercise includes undertaking prayer and action that condition its leadership, membership, and governing practices (a) to tolerate dissent and diversity within its ranks, (b) to change and adapt over time, and (c) to recognize and honestly speak about and correct what is destructive and inauthentic. Prior to World War II, Professor Reinhold Niebuhr noted that institutions, even using that term loosely, find difficult any tasks and challenges that do not prop up and reinforce their particular group.[20] A crucial task for any "institution" desiring genuine, holistic health, then, is to encourage adding objectivity to the lives and judgments of individuals within the "body of the institution" to counter our overwhelmingly subjective tendencies.

2. *Can communities of faith be nonsectarian in their discipleship and mission without surrendering their distinctiveness and becoming simply part of the wider culture?* Late-twentieth- and early-twenty-first-century folk are not the first ones to ask this question. The question has been posed and the question has been explored in the lives of God's people across the centuries. Of particular interest to us, however, may be some of the lines penned by German Lutheran Dietrich Bonhoeffer, whose life, discipleship, and imprisonment were mentioned previously. He was executed April 9, 1945. Almost exactly a year prior to his execution, Bonhoeffer wrote honestly, yet with a tone approaching apprehension, to his friend and relative by marriage, Eberhard Bethge:

You would be surprised, and perhaps even worried, by my theological thoughts and the conclusions that they lead to. . . . What is bothering me incessantly is the question what Christianity really is, or indeed who Christ really is, for us today. . . . We are moving towards a completely religionless time; people, as they are now simply cannot be religious anymore. . . . If our final judgment must be that the Western form of Christianity . . . was only a preliminary stage to a complete absence of religion, what kind of situation emerges for us, for the church? How can Christ become the Lord of the religionless as well? Are there religionless Christians? If religion is only a garment of Christianity—and even this garment has looked very different at different times—then what is a religionless Christianity?[21]

Bonhoeffer then notes in his letter how Karl Barth began a wider discussion of "religionless Christianity," but, Bonhoeffer states, Barth did not develop this thought-line in a helpful way. Bonhoeffer opines that Professor Barth, rather, reverted to a doctrine of revelation that reinforced church tradition, even though that reinforcement may have been done in a way that was somewhat new, calling for a different theological perspective. Bonhoeffer may have been saying that Barth's critiques changed theology more than those critiques changed the sociology of humans as God's people in communities with one another. Bonhoeffer then continues:

> What do a church, a community, a sermon, a liturgy, a Christian life mean in a religionless world? . . . In what way are we "religionless—secular" Christians, in what way are we the *Ekklesia*, those who are called forth, not regarding ourselves from a religious point of view as specially favored, but rather belonging wholly to the world? In that case, Christ is no longer an object of religion, but something quite different, really the Lord of the world.[22]

Bonhoeffer's ponderings from a prison cell, not knowing if or when he might be executed, are equally questions of our time and culture even when we're not in prison. His questions become relevant for us as the people whom we encounter in the twenty-first century lose interest in traditional religious practices (a time labeled by some as "postdenominational").

He ponders what the Christian faith would be like if and when relieved of its institutional weight (church tradition and hierarchy in its variety of specific forms). In July 1944, he wrote:

> I suppose I wrote *The Cost of Discipleship* as the end of a path seeking to acquire faith by trying to live a holy life. Today I can see the dangers of that book, though I still stand by what I wrote. I discovered later, and I'm still discovering right up to this moment, that it is only by living completely in this world that one learns to have faith. One must completely abandon any attempt to make something of oneself, whether it be a saint, or a converted sinner, or a churchman (a so-called priestly type!), a righteous person or an unrighteous one, a sick person or a healthy one. . . . In so doing, we throw ourselves completely into the arms of God, taking seriously, not our own sufferings, but those of God in the world. . . . Watching with Christ in Gethsemane. That, I think, is faith; that is metanoia (the Greek word for "repentance" and "change of direction"); and that is how one becomes a person and a Christian.[23]

About that same time, still from prison, Bonhoeffer was writing a book outline. Two sentences in that outline stand out, the first: "The church is the church only when it exists for others." Second: "The church must tell persons of every calling (and life situation) what it means to live in Christ, to exist for others."

Bonhoeffer was quite possibly deeply affected by his experience of what he judged to be the acquiescence of the German Christian Church to the Nazi regime. As an active dissenter, then, he was convinced that the church will be more faithful when it is less interested and less on-task with efforts to maintain and preserve itself institutionally. He was also very clear that the being and the mission of God's people *as disciples of Jesus* will always have legitimacy following Jesus.

That Bonhoeffer wrote such words from a prison cell in Germany in 1945 is almost hard to imagine. The words sound incredibly contemporary. In the year 2001, church as an institution or as religious communities in more congregational and somewhat less institutional manifestations still are attractive to some, even to many persons. In American culture, though, this attractiveness seems reduced from the post–World War II years. Those years at least seemed to be "fat-cow measuring-stick-years" for many mainline and economically middle- and upper-class religious institutions in the United States.

People in our North American context attracted to religious institutions often look for a presence of authority as much as for a presence of "the sacred" or "the holy" in one's life. Others do not find institutions attractive, and particularly not religious institutions. The acquiescence to authority that those institutions might ask of "believers," "adherents," or "members" is simply too much to ask of many twenty-first-century people, North Americans in particular. Also, while the desire is for a spirituality touched by "the sacred" or "what is holy," many twenty-first-century persons would simply conclude that other, more meaningful ways are available for each one respectively to be in touch with and to experience "the sacred" or "the holy" apart from institutional religious communities.

FOUR FOOTINGS FOR ECCENTRIC DISCIPLES OF JESUS

If someone asks, "What do eccentric, nonsectarian disciples of Jesus believe?" then, even in a dot.com world and postmodern ethos, we can say that in some way or another, today's disciples of Jesus are convinced

1. *of the Lordship of Jesus Christ,* meaning Jesus of Nazareth is the one in whom God fully reveals a picture as complete as we will see;

2. *of the ministry of Word and sacrament,* meaning that both Scripture and sacraments (such as baptism and the Lord's Supper) are important symbols and vessels of God's magnificent grace among God's people. Scripture and sacraments are entrusted to the church. We say that God's word becomes flesh in Jesus and that God's spirit further speaks through the Scriptures of faith communities and is present in the celebrations of sacraments. *Word* and *sacrament,* therefore, continually function both as reminders and center-points around which our lives both revolve and evolve as members and participants in communities of faith. Through the years, God's center-points of Word and sacrament exert certain influences (similar to the sun's pull of gravity), moving us (as God's people). Such moving both shapes and moves us for maturity by grace.

3. *of the stewardship of life* to which we are called, mentally, emotionally, economically, relationally, in areas of science, the arts, service, research, development, production, caring, politics, governing, etc.

4. *of the communion of saints,* meaning not that some of God's people stand a rung or two higher than others on the ladder of God's favor, but that each person—both with one's life and service in ministry, as a person of God—is always connected to the life and ministry of others around the globe at any given moment, as well as being connected to the life and service in ministry of God's people centuries before.

You might disagree with this list of four. Your list might be longer, or shorter, or the same length yet different. In a community of faith unafraid of dialogue, diversity, and disagreement, we'll still be neighbors (even sisters and brothers) because the community can "breathe" by the eccentric, nonsectarian grace of God.

SUPPLIES FOR EXAMINATIONS, RESEARCH, AND ANALYSIS

Prior to beginning your journey through the Great Canyon, be sure to check your supplies for what you will observe, encounter, and experience on the journey. (Other canyon guides may recommend different "supplies" for the journey. Feel free to ask others or to write your own list, but, for the moment, you seem to have your hand extended to receive our supply list.) We think it's important, and we recommend, that you carry with you:

(1) reverence; (2) curiosity; (3) honesty; (4) passion; (5) reasonableness; (6) awe; and (7) patience.

1. *Reverence* equips a person and group with an abiding respect: for the Holy One who is God; for the known and unknown, the explainable and the unexplainable in God's world; for other human beings; for one's self; and for all of creation.
2. *Curiosity* equips a person or group for inquiry, which always takes one beyond accepting information or conclusions simply because another person "says it's so."
3. *Honesty* equips a person and group for evaluating with forthrightness and candor one's gifts, strengths, vulnerabilities, and failings, as well as equipping persons for greater objectivity in investigations and assessments.
4. *Passion* equips a person and group for being engaged with energy, conviction, and a sense of abiding purpose. Passion can be a primary contributor to a person's and group's willingness and ability to persevere when subjected to adversity or persecution.
5. *Reasonableness* equips a person and group for accepting varying contexts, situations, perspectives, and data as valid even though one might not have acknowledged those as valid at an earlier point in time.
6. *Awe* equips a person and group for appreciating mystery, simplicity, intricacy, variety, complexity, and sacredness in life, and to appreciate without needing to attempt gaining control.
7. *Patience* equips a person and group for attitudes and conduct that view life as evolving day by day. Patience honors process and processes as being usual and normative. ("Rome wasn't built in a day!") Patience avoids obsessiveness and fretting over every mistake and every appearance, sign, and evidence of incompleteness. Any person's life and any part of life as creation and history can be understood as part of a larger "whole," not as an end in oneself or as an end unto itself.

PULLING MUCH TOGETHER

In May 1944, less than two weeks before the Allied forces invaded western Europe to break the stranglehold of Germany's Third Reich regime, a gathering was held in New York City's Central Park. One hundred and fifty thousand persons took the oath of citizenship there. Among the speakers that day was Federal Judge Learned Hand. He is said to have given the briefest speech, less than five hundred words, and likely the most memorable, including these sentences:

> What do we mean when we say that first of all we seek liberty? Liberty lies in the hearts of men and women; when it dies there, no constitution, no law, no court can save it; no constitution, no law, no court can even do much to help it. . . . Liberty is not freedom to do as one likes. That is the denial of liberty, and leads straight to overthrow. A society in which (persons) recognize no check upon their freedom soon becomes a society where freedom is the possession of only a savage few; as we have learned to our sorrow. . . . What then is the spirit of liberty? I cannot define it; I can only tell you my own faith. The spirit of liberty is the spirit which is not too sure that it is right; the spirit of liberty is the spirit which seeks to understand the minds of other men and women; the spirit of liberty is the spirit which weighs their interests alongside its own without bias; the spirit of liberty remembers that not even a sparrow falls to earth unheeded; the spirit of liberty is the spirit of Him who, near two thousand years ago, taught (humankind) that lesson it has never learned, but has never quite forgotten; that there may be a kingdom where the least shall be heard and considered side by side with the greatest.[24]

Judge Hand's brief speech about liberty and citizenship describes with memorable phrases much of what we believe is essential and possible for a faithful and eccentric discipleship following Jesus. This Jesus is the one who fulfills the words of the Teachings and the faithful Prophets from the Hebrew Scriptures, as well as the Second (New) Testament, representing God who journeys with God's people across the ages through the Great Canyon, which is always east of Eden.

While we human beings may not have an earthly existence forever as a species of creation, we are more adaptable than thylacine to the challenges facing us. In the face and in the midst of every challenge, God's grace calls us to be and grow both as persons and as a larger community without being institutionally captive to culture: not religious culture, national, ethnic, generational, or any other sort.

Now for the question in the title of this chapter: "Can disciples of Jesus exist as SOTMOGs outside of institutional captivity?" Yes, with this qualification: Disciples of Jesus do not operate outside of community. The biblical tradition itself is based on God's involvement with communities of persons. It is possible, paraphrasing Jesus, to be "in the institution" without being "of the institution." By God's grace it is possible to be part of an institutional structure without being captive to its institutionally self-serving and self-preserving tendencies. Dietrich Bonhoeffer, for example, was paradoxically a SOTMOG in prison who was, even then—more than most persons are—free from institutional captivity (!) by either church culture or state culture.

To paraphrase English writer Richard Lovelace,[25] "We can be captives without being locked behind any wall or fence or window bars; and, theoretically, when locked behind walls, fences, and window bars, we can be more free than captive." Our condition all depends on our openness to being shaped by God's word and spirit, beyond the pressures and temptations to support cultural institutions simply so those institutions can continue in the forms with which they are most comfortable.

We can do that, negotiating the trails between chaotic abysses and oppressive labyrinths, affirming the Lordship of Jesus Christ, the ministry of Word and sacrament, the stewardship of life, and the communion of saints. As stewards of the mysteries of God, without being captive to any institution, we are prepared and accompanied eccentrically by God's gracious word and spirit. The journey lasts all through life and across the centuries, and is an experience with a joyful component, no matter how complex, challenging, even agonizing, the journey ever turns out to be.

That's why and how, even in a dot.com world and postmodern ethos, we are able to take the first step and every step thereafter, not simply as individuals but with others as members of faith communities. That's how and why, even in cultures seeking conformity, we can be willing to be damned. We'll find ourselves being willing when that being damned would bring glory and honor to that nonconformist One who is said initially to have met human beings inside a garden called Eden, and who, centuries afterward, in the person and ministry of Jesus, met folk "out" in regions called Galilee and Samaria and elsewhere.

That same One has met us ever since, wherever any happen to be, beyond Eden's (locked) eastern gate, and always will meet us along the trails of the Great Canyon that is life.

While we're hiking, we can even join in song. Here are some of the words we might sing (to the tune of "The Battle Hymn of the Republic"):

Would you become a SOTMOG, by God's grace which calls to you?
Serve with stewards of the mysteries of God the ages through?

Hear God's faithful are eccentric as God seeks to make life new?
No number is too few!
(Refrain) With humility and courage, in community and grateful,
Foll'wing Jesus' way and spirit, may we to God be true!

NOTES AND JOURNALING OPPORTUNITIES

I.   Parts of this chapter with which I have mostly agreed in the past:

II. Parts of this chapter with which I have mostly disagreed in the past:

III. Parts of this chapter which have presented new thoughts or information for me:

IV. What's in this chapter . . .

(a) prompts me to remember

(b) prompts me, from years past, to wonder about

(c) prompts me to want to ask, to investigate, to research

(d) prompts me to wonder about changing

(e) prompts me to wonder about the near future in the following ways

(f) prompts me to wonder about the more distant future in the following ways

V. Personal writings, sketches, drawings related to this chapter

Epilogue

A poor man in a village went every day down to the river to collect water for the day. He carried two jars on a pole in which to gather the water. Because he was poor, his jars were far from perfect as there were slight cracks in each of their sides. And every day as the man went to collect the water along the long, winding path leading to the river, he would fill each jar and on his return to the village, the cracked jars always leaked over half their water through the cracks. The poor man felt badly that he was failing to do his duty for the village since he was always losing so much water through the cracked jars and could not afford new perfect vessels in which to carry the water. Every day for many years he would trudge down to the river, fill the vessels with water, and hurry back to the village, but every time the water would leak out along the way. He worried over this imperfection, for there was often barely enough water to last the day because so much had been lost along the path.

One day he shared his dilemma with the village mother, who only smiled and shook her head. "My son," she said, "do not be anxious. For as you have walked these many years along the path, water leaking from your imperfect jars, go and see what God has done." The puzzled poor water carrier went back to the long winding path and saw something he had not expected. For all along the path where the water had leaked these many years, beautiful flowers had grown nourished by the spilled water from the cracked jars. And the man began to dance among the flowers.

The church is those cracked jars. Many people are anxious that the church has failed to be the perfect vessel in which to carry the living water of Jesus Christ to the world. Yet, somehow God has grown much beauty out of this water leaking from our cracks. Can we realize that we are not called to perfection as we tend to define perfection, but to be the imperfect vessels from which God's grace can leak out into the world? In fact, one can say, by our cracks grace truly flows freely.

We are called in our imperfect spiritual lives to be grace-full. We are called to trust that God will create beauty out of the grace that leaks from our broken lives, for when we trust God's grace, we are set free to be the authentic and vulnerable community God creates in the world called the church. It is good news indeed that God's grace is not dependent upon us, but more that we are dependent on God's grace.

Where can we find Jesus in this chaotic and strange world of the twenty-first century? Jesus can be found all along the long, winding path inviting us to dance among the flowers of God's grace. Jesus is in the world in ways mysterious and surprising, among people and places we have not and frequently will not expect or anticipate. Jesus is inviting us to dance. And when we are grace-full, we dance!

We dance wherever God's gift of grace is celebrated and not sold. We dance wherever there is the humility to know we are all cracked vessels. We dance where there is such gratitude that only in dancing can we express it. We dance wherever a community of people loves and celebrates the "other." We dance wherever there is the courage to be eccentric in the midst of a broken world.

Where is Jesus in a dot.com world? He is right alongside us, though we often fail to see him. But every now and then, we hear his call and see his face. "Come follow me," he says. "Come dance with me." Shall we dance?

Appendix

Suggestions for Class or Discussion Group Leaders

We admit to a general preference for inductive learning rather than for a dominant "diet" of deductive learning. Given that preference, we suggest that readers may find it helpful (as individuals or when reading these chapters as part of a group) to use the journaling pages provided at the end of each chapter.

Also, group/class coordinators may give an advance assignment to the group. The goal of an advance assignment is to allow for additional time in research or creative thought. The fruits of such an effort can both kick off some aspect of the group discussion in the next gathering and maximize the group's time. Such advance assignments may also increase the interest and participation of group members. This advance assignment

- may relate to a part of the journaling page for the particular chapter;
- may originate from the "Discussion and Activity Possibilities" for the chapter being read;
- may be something entirely different from either of the preceding suggestions;
- may be a request of the entire group, or may be an invitation that asks for a volunteer or volunteers, rather than seeking the advance work of the entire group.

DISCUSSION AND ACTIVITY POSSIBILITIES

1. A group/class coordinator may be the same individual throughout the multiple weeks of the study period. Another option is to rotate leadership of the presentations. See (4.) and (5.) below.

2. A group/class coordinator is encouraged to begin each gathering by introducing regular class members and guests/newcomers. The leader/coordinator then may ask how life is going for participants since the last gathering and if there are particular prayer requests. If beginning with a general prayer, the coordinator may include a brief reference both to the prayer requests and to chapter subject material. We recommend that any sentence (or two) related to the study material be prepared ahead of time by the coordinator, much like a book of liturgy suggests a certain "collect" prayer for particular Sundays of the church calendar year.

3. A group/class coordinator may ask participants what questions and comments they want to offer about the chapter (perhaps from their journaling pages) and what they want to make sure is out on the table for consideration as the class begins. (Coordinators are encouraged to utilize newsprint, chalkboard, erasable marker board, or overhead projector to write these questions and comments so they are visible to participants.)

4. A group/class coordinator may design, prepare in advance, copy, and distribute a one-page skeleton outline of the chapter to facilitate discussion. Related passages of Scripture may be noted on the outline for reference during the discussion period or for participants to consult following their time together.

5. A group/class coordinator may walk through the chapter outline, briefly summarizing the chapter and highlighting major points within the chapter. ("Briefly" means no more than ten to fifteen minutes.) Group/class coordinators are encouraged not to include strong personal opinions in such summarizing efforts. We make this suggestion not because the authors are more correct than anyone else, but so that class members will feel maximum freedom to speak about their own opinions and wonderings following the coordinator's summary.

6. Following any brief summary presentation, options vary for the remainder of time allowed (which probably needs to be at least half of the class period).

- The group/class coordinator may refer to the group's questions previously put on the table (see [3.] above), and discussion may begin from there.
- The group/class may use a combination of activities and questions, some possibilities of which are printed here. The group or class may remain as one group or may break into subgroups of three or four people each for consideration of the questions or the activities. (The four questions here suggested for each chapter are merely

samples. The first one or two can be distinguished as "text-specific" and the others as more "reflection–probing/wondering." Note: A most helpful resource readily available is a section entitled, "The Art of Asking Questions," in Don Griggs's *Teaching Teachers to Teach: A Basic Manual for Church Teachers,* (Nashville: Abingdon, 1980).

INTRODUCTION

1. In the opinion of the authors, what are the four "essential indicators" of God's grace?

2. What does *la lucha* mean?

3. What differences are there between the questions, "Where is God?" and "Is there a God?"

4. What inconsistencies or disconnects have you noticed or thought about between (a) what you've been taught concerning the Bible and the Christian faith and (b) real life, as you or others experience real life?

5. The group time may be concluded with a brief prayer or the singing of a hymn or spiritual song.

CHAPTER 1

1. What is a helpful definition of "ethos"?

2. What are working definitions or understandings of (a) premodernist? (b) modernist? (c) postmodernist?

3. What experiences have you had or what observations have you made that led you to wonder if "church" is, in fact, primarily trying to "make people feel good" or "feel better"?

4. What's an experience you could describe when your faith "foundation slab" began to crack? Did grace (in any form) help or strengthen at that time, or since? If so, describe how.

5. The group time may be concluded with a brief prayer or the singing of a hymn or spiritual song.

CHAPTER 2

1. What is anti-Semitism? In the way that the authors describe the German Christian Church buying into the anti-Semitism of the Nazi regime, what culturally conditioned values—in the present—are you asked, pressured, or encouraged to buy into or endorse?

2. What definition of "eccentric" do the authors suggest?

3. Think of (a) Hitler, (b) Gandhi, (c) Marilyn Monroe, (d) St. Francis of Assisi, (e) Dorothy Day, (f) Britney Spears, (g) John Wayne, (h) Cesar Chavez, (i) Thurgood Marshall, (j) Ozzy Osbourne. (Other names may be used in place of or in addition to these suggested.) Do their lives variously give more evidence of conforming to a culture or of transforming culture and being transformed in the midst of a culture?

4. How does the movie *Chocolat,* as described, indicate that eccentricity breaks certain cultural molds? What does a healthy eccentricity embrace or affirm that's wonderful and worthy of celebrating?

5. The group time may be concluded with a brief prayer or the singing of a hymn or spiritual song.

CHAPTER 3

1. Describe eBay, hypercapitalism, and hyperconsumerism.

2. What is "grace" as in "God's grace in life"?

3. Divide group members to prepare a brief (ninety-second) argument, one side arguing "for" the following proposition and one side arguing "against": "God's grace is free and therefore costs nothing."

Afterward, discuss what was said in the debate. Is there a difference between "costly" and "expensive" as contrasted with "price-less"?

4. Ask group members (individually or in small groups) to write a brief (one to five sentences) "elder son epilogue" to the story Jesus tells in Luke 15:11–32. This might be another, later scene/episode or a letter/speech/ diary entry by the elder son addressed either to his dad or younger brother. It may be rap, free or rhymed verse, or straight narrative. Discuss these as time allows.

5. The group time may be concluded with a brief prayer or the singing of a hymn or spiritual song.

CHAPTER 4

1. What are working definitions for (a) "humility" and (b) "triumphalism"?

2. Remembering that God's grace includes both God's justice and God's mercy, how can God's grace create humility?

3. Ask the entire group, or divide into small groups of three or four, to list reasons that they might agree and disagree with the following statement: "Low self-esteem plus aggressiveness in one person's life yields oppression for someone else."

4. Group members may be asked to remember and tell (either to the entire group or to a subgroup) about persons whom they have known who were (are) both respectful and bold, or put another way, who were (are) both humble and self-confident.

5. The group time may be concluded with a brief prayer or the singing of a hymn or spiritual song.

CHAPTER 5

1. What is a working definition for "gratitude"? Group members might be asked to tell stories or experiences of what they have been taught in the past about gratitude (positively and negatively) as they recall what others have said (family members, colleagues, church leaders, some aspect of the culture, etc.). Examples might be the beer commercial that encouraged, "Go for the gusto," the saying, "I don't owe you anything," and others.

2. Group members might be asked to pick two of the "Immensa Gratia" pinball posts as favorites. In small groups of two or three (or as a group if the large group is manageable), participants might tell about their favorites. The group might also be asked, "If you could add a seventh and eighth 'post' to the game playing surface, how would you describe them?"

3. If "everything is stewardship," and persons face various (even multiple) challenges, choose two or three below and discuss what differences exist in stewardship for the following people: (a) a high school student; (b) an adult in his or her early twenties; (c) a single person "early" in a career; (d) younger adults married but without children; (e) two parents with very young children; (f) two parents with school-age children; (g) a single parent; (h) parents with one or more "special needs" daughters or sons; (i) "retirement age" adults, single or married; (j) adults in "upper senior" years.

4. Group members can be invited to write a poem, prayer, story, "reflective sentences," etc., on the subject of gratitude and our relationship to God—past, present, or future.

5. The group time may be concluded with a brief prayer or the singing of a hymn or spiritual song.

CHAPTER 6

1. What feelings does a person have when hoping to succeed and then fumbling the opportunity?

2. What are some of the factors creating situations when persons "vote against" someone else in a "*Survivor's* world"?

3. As in the story of the man asking questions and Jesus responding by telling the parable of The Good Samaritan (Luke 10:25–37), what are some reasons we try to justify ourselves?

4. How would group/class members respond to this question: Can you describe a situation when you thought there would be no chance of a community developing but something happened and a sense of community did develop?

5. The group time may be concluded with a brief prayer or the singing of a hymn or spiritual song.

CHAPTER 7

1. What is positive and helpful about McDonald's, Burger King, and other fast-service businesses?

2. What is positive about churches being efficient and predictable?

3. If someone said, "I think our church ought to spend more time in the effort of running a soup kitchen," or "We need to have more adults involved in the tutoring program at the neighborhood elementary school," someone else might say, "But we never receive any new members through those ministries." How do you respectfully respond to the person making the latter statement?

4. How do you think that courage "happens"? Is a person born with courage? Is courage taught? Is courage a matter of instinct? Is courage a reflex action? Is courage predictable or unpredictable? Is courage a response for which persons somehow can be prepared over a period of time? What are some ways through which you've been prepared to respond with courage when pressured to "go along in order to get along"?

5. The group time may be concluded with a brief prayer or the singing of a hymn or spiritual song.

CHAPTER 8—PART I

1. What are working definitions for: (a) hermeneutic? (b) ecclesiology? (c) *jihad*? (d) SOTMOG?

2. Group members may be asked: "Express 'likes' and 'dislikes' with respect to the varied endings of Bernard Malamud's 1952 book, *The Natural*, and the 1984 movie with the same name."

3. Group members may be invited to tell of an experience in the past (with persons in settings such as school, work, family, church, community) through which a person or group essentially said, "Believing this way is

required for being accepted as part of this group." In the instances recalled, what resulted from this sort of requirement?

4. The authors ask the question: "Does faith stay 'simple' and does faith create 'good feelings' every time faith is known or experienced?" Group members may be asked to respond: How would you answer that two-part question: (a) "yes" to both parts; (b) "no" to both parts; (c) "yes" to "simple" and "no" to "good feelings"; (d) "no" to "simple" and "yes" to "good feelings"? What thoughts or experiences contribute to your opinion?

5. The group time may be concluded with a brief prayer or the singing of a hymn or spiritual song.

CHAPTER 8—PART II

1. What is a thylacine? What other creatures have become extinct because of humans' aggressive encroachment and insensitivity? What tends to happen when cultural groups (including religious groups) become so focused on their own interests that they feel threatened by others who are eccentric in their faithfulness? (In other words, do we see that the response of the Tasmanian livestock ranchers and shepherds to the thylacine is repeated wherever members of a given group feel overly threatened and respond with little attention to the integrity of others?)

2. Invite group members to tell from personal experience, or from what may have been learned and recalled from history, of a time when "church" has "behaved badly."

3. The authors list "four footings" that eccentric, nonsectarian disciples of Jesus might consider crucial. How would group members change or add to that list?

4. Do group members agree or disagree that disciples of Jesus in a dot.com world can exist as SOTMOGs and as church members and officers, and yet not be captives of the institutionalizing pressures of "church"? If any group members agree that this is possible, who could they name from personal life experience or from history that would help convince them? In what ways would group members describe those whom they name as being either "faithfully eccentric" or "eccentric in faithfulness"? Ask if they might tell what they have observed in those persons' lives that could be described as "faithfully eccentric" or "eccentric in faithfulness."

5. The group time may be concluded with a brief prayer or the singing of a hymn or spiritual song.

Notes

INTRODUCTION

1. Ted V. Foote Jr. and P. Alex Thornburg, *Being Presbyterian in the Bible Belt* (Louisville, Ky.: Geneva Press, 2000).
2. Karl Barth, *The Word of God and the Word of Man*, trans. Douglas Horton (New York: Harper and Row, 1957), 51–58.
3. John B. Rogers Jr., "The Book That Reads Us," *Interpretation* 39 (Richmond: Union Theological Seminary, October 1985), 388–411.

CHAPTER 1
IS POSTMODERNISM REAL, OR ARE WE JUST MAKING IT UP?

1. *The Wizard of Oz* (1939), directed by Victor Fleming, written by Noel Langley, Florence Ryerson, Edgar Allen Woolf: Metro Goldwyn Mayer Studios.
2. This story was related to one of the authors by a seminary classmate.
3. A number of theologians have made this observation, among them Dr. Paul Dietrich of the Center for Parish Development, an organization that takes seriously the cultural contexts and the church's faithful responses in ministry. The *Center for Parish Development Newsletter*, Chicago.
4. *Random House Dictionary of the English Language: College Edition* (New York: Random House, 1968), 454.
5. Stanley J. Grenz, *A Primer on Postmodernism* (Grand Rapids: William B. Eerdmans Publishing, 1996), 2–3, 57–81.
6. Ibid., 11–38.
7. Ibid., 2, 5–43.
8. Personal correspondence (edited) to P. Alex Thornburg and Ted V. Foote Jr., authors of the book that Laura's letter mentions, *Being Presbyterian in the Bible Belt*.

CHAPTER 2
IS GOD ECCENTRIC OR COMFORTABLY MIDDLE CLASS?

1. A Presbyterian Church (U.S.A.) minister, the Reverend John Nelsen, has been heard saying this, as, no doubt, others (including non-Presbyterians) have also said or thought it.
2. Daniel Jonah Goldhagen, *Hitler's Willing Executioners: Ordinary Germans and the Holocaust* (New York: Vintage Books/Random House, 1997).
3. Ibid., 49–128.
4. Ibid., 119–124.
5. Ibid., 106.
6. Ibid., 107.
7. Ibid., 126.
8. Ibid., 113. See also, Eberhard Busch, *Karl Barth: His Life from Letters and Autobiographical Texts* (Philadelphia: Fortress Press, 1976), 234–35.
9. Goldhagen, 114.
10. Stanley Hauerwas and William H. Willimon, *Resident Aliens* (Nashville: Abingdon Press, 1989).
11. The reason we may be off center is that we revolve around a different center, namely, Jesus Christ.
12. David Weeks and Jamie James, *Eccentrics: A Study of Sanity and Strangeness* (New York: Villard/Random House, 1995).
13. Ibid., 247–55.
14. *Chocolat* (2000), directed by Lasse Hallström, screenplay by Robert Nelson Jacobs: Miramax Films, from a novel with the same name by Joanne Harris (New York: Penguin Press/Putnam, 1999).

CHAPTER 3
HOW MUCH IS GRACE, OR IS IT JUST CHEAP?

1. Victor Hugo, *Les Miserables*, trans. Charles E. Wilbour (New York: Fawcett Premier, 1961, 1987), 1–39.
2. Bruce Wilkinson, *The Prayer of Jabez* (Sisters, Oreg.: Multnomah Publishers, 2000). Many people find this little book on prayer provocative and helpful. We would particularly emphasize that there is a way to interpret this prayer by which we who pray ask God to challenge us daily beyond what we would consider doing ourselves. One needs equally to perceive, though, that prayer is not dependent on our asking God for something as if God's blessings can be dependent on our asking or acting. Blessings are gifts. Period.
3. Philip Yancey, *What's So Amazing about Grace?* (Grand Rapids: Zondervan Publishing House, 1977), 12.
4. Dietrich Bonhoeffer, *The Cost of Discipleship*, trans. R. H. Fuller and Irmgard Booth (New York, Macmillan Publishing, 1945, 1976).

5. Ibid., 45.
6. Phil. 2:6–8.
7. Bonhoeffer, *Cost of Discipleship*, 99.

CHAPTER 4
CAN WE HANG WITH THE NAMES ON JESUS' BUDDY LIST?

1. Mac Davis, "It's Hard to Be Humble," on the CD, *Baby, Don't Get Hooked on Me / Stop and Smell the Roses* (Golden Classics Edition, 1997).
2. Olive Ann Burns, *Cold Sassy Tree* (New York: Dell Publishing, 1984), 189.
3. Davis, "It's Hard to Be Humble."
4. Daniel J. Boorstin, *The Discoverers: A History of Man's Search to Know His World and Himself* (New York: Vintage/Random House, 1985), 294–327; and Edward O. Wilson, *Consilience: The Unity of Knowledge* (New York: Vintage/Random House, 1998, 1999), 35.
5. See Jonathan Z. Smith, *Drudgery Divine: On the Comparison of Early Christianities and the Religions of Late Antiquity* (Chicago: University of Chicago Press, 1990).
6. Peter DeVries, *The Mackerel Plaza* (1959; reprint, New York: Viking/Penguin, 1986), 1–5.
7. Carl Sandburg, "How the Potato Face Blind Man Enjoyed Himself on a Fine Spring Morning," in *Rootabaga Stories* (1922; reprint; Bedford, Mass.: Appleseed Books, 1996), 46.
8. Mark Harris, *Bang the Drum Slowly* (1956; reprint, Lincoln: University of Nebraska Press, 1984), 140.

CHAPTER 5
WHAT WOULD JESUS DRIVE?

1. Julie Delcour, "WWJD: What Would Jesus Drive?" in *The Tulsa World*, January 6, 2002.
2. Texas Presbyterian elder Wayne Fahle has said this over and over, possibly quoting someone else, possibly quoting himself; and we think he's correct.
3. See also, Ps. 8:6–8.
4. Walter Brueggemann, *Genesis,* Interpretation (Atlanta: John Knox Press, 1982), 32–33.
5. Ibid.
6. Delcour, "WWJD."
7. Ibid.
8. Ibid.
9. Robert Lee III, in a sermon preached at John Calvin Presbyterian Church, Tulsa, Okla., February 3, 2002 ("Youth" Sunday).

10. Charles D. Warner, quoted in *The International Dictionary of Thoughts*, ed. J. P. Bradley, L. F. Daniels, and T. C. Jones (Chicago: J. G. Ferguson Pubishing, 1969), 668.
11. Kendall C. Foote, in a sermon preached at John Calvin Presbyterian Church, Tulsa, Okla., February 3, 2002 ("Youth" Sunday).
12. John Milbank, "Why Did Christ Die?" two addresses delivered as the guest lecturer of the 2002 Snuggs Lectures in Religion, The University of Tulsa, Tulsa, Okla., April 2–3, 2002.
13. Willie Morris, *Taps* (Boston: Houghton Mifflin, 2001), 336–38.
14. Anthony Godby Johnson, *A Rock and a Hard Place: One Boy's Triumphant Story* (New York: Crown Publishing, 1993), 211.
15. Inscribed on a stone panel in the gathering hall of National Presbyterian Church, Washington, D.C.

CHAPTER 6
AM I MY SIBLINGS' KEEPER, OR ARE THEY THE WEAKEST LINKS?

1. Phillip C. McGraw, *Self Matters: Creating Your Life from the Inside Out* (New York: Simon and Schuster, 2001).
2. Robert Bellah, Richard Madsen, William M. Sullivan, Ann Swidler, and Steven M. Tipton, *Habits of the Heart: Individualism and Commitment in American Life* (New York: Harper and Row, 1985), 218.
3. Such alliances are equally part of a *Survivor* "cousin-show," the studio-based *Weakest Link*.
4. *Grand Canyon* (1991), directed by Lawrence Kasdan, written by Lawrence Kasdan and Meg Kasdan: 20th Century Fox.
5. Gen. 4:9.

CHAPTER 7
"HAVE IT YOUR WAY" OR "WE LOVE TO SEE YOU SMILE"?

1. John F. Kennedy, *Profiles in Courage* (1956; reprint, New York: Harper Collins, 2000), 1.
2. Philip Hallie, *Lest Innocent Blood Be Shed: The Story of the Village of Le Chambon and How Goodness Happened There* (New York: Harper and Row, 1979).
3. George Ritzer, *The McDonaldization of Society* (Thousand Oaks, Calif.: Pine Forge Press, 1993), 1.
4. Ibid., 36–82.
5. Ibid., 82–99.
6. Ibid., 100–120.
7. Marva Dawn, *A Royal Waste of Time: The Splender of Worshiping God and Being Church for the World* (Grand Rapids: William B. Eerdmans Publishing, 1999).

CHAPTER 8
CAN SOTMOGS EXIST OUTSIDE OF INSTITUTIONAL CAPTIVITY?

1. Dallas M. Roark, *Dietrich Bonhoeffer*, Makers of the Modern Theological Mind, ed. Bob E. Patterson (Waco, Tex.: Word Books, 1972), 21–25.
2. Alan Bullock, *Hitler: A Study in Tyranny*, rev. ed. (1962; reprint, New York: Harper and Row, 1964), 743–44.
3. Roark, 24–25.
4. Dietrich Bonhoeffer, *Letters and Papers from Prison: The Enlarged Edition*, ed. Eberhard Bethge (1953; reprint, New York: Macmillan Publishing, 1975).
5. Roark, 26–29.
6. Bullock, 744.
7. Bernard Malamud, *The Natural* (1952; reprint, New York: Avon, 1982).
8. *The Natural* (1984), directed by Barry Levinson, written by Roger Towne and Phil Dusenberry: Tri-Star Pictures.
9. Malamud, *The Natural*, 243–62.
10. Van A. Harvey, *A Handbook of Theological Terms* (1964; reprint, New York: Macmillan Publishing, 1978), 117–18.
11. See the Scots Confession (1550), printed in *The Constitution of the Presbyterian Church (U.S.A.)*, Part I, *Book of Confessions*, 3.16.
12. See Byron L. Haines and Frank L. Cooley, eds., *Christians and Muslims Together: An Exploration by Presbyterians* (Philadelphia: Geneva Press, 1987), 24; and Ben and Carol Weir, with Dennis Benson, *Hostage Bound, Hostage Free* (Philadelphia: Westminster Press, 1987), 61.
13. Jouette M. Basslar, "I Corinthians 4:1–5," *Interpretation* 44 (Richmond: Union Theological Seminary, April 1990), 181.
14. David Macdonald, ed., "Thylacine," in *The Encyclopedia of Mammals* (1984; reprint, New York: Andromeda/Oxford, 1993), 841.
15. C. Campbell's NaturalWorlds.org (Web site), "Tasmanian Wolf," from *Grzimek's Animal Life Encyclopedia* (New York: Van Nostrand Reinhold, 1972–75), 4; see also, Dr. Bernard Grzimek's *Grzimek's Animal Life Encyclopedia* (New York: Van Nostrand Reinhold, 1984), vol. 10, 83–96.
16. See Mary Douglas, "Justice As the Cornerstone: An Interpretation of Leviticus 18–20," *Interpretation*, 53 (Richmond: Union Theological Seminary, October 1999), 341–50; and Robert Oden, "The Ideal Cultic Order: The Holiness Code and the Priestly Work," Lecture 15 of *The Old Testament: An Introduction, Part II*, 2d ed. (Springfield, Va.: The Teaching Company, 1997); videotape.
17. *The Constitution of the Presbyterian Church (U.S.A.)*, Part II, *Book of Order*, G-2.0500a.(4)
18. William J. Bousma, *John Calvin: A Sixteenth-Century Portrait* (New York: Oxford University Press, 1988), 45–48.
19. William Morris, ed., *The American Heritage Dictionary of the English Language* (Boston: Houghton Mifflin, 1978), 1173.

20. See Reinhold Niebuhr, *Moral Man and Immoral Society: A Study in Ethics and Politics* (1932; reprint, New York: Simon and Schuster, 1976).
21. Bonhoeffer, *Letters and Papers*, 280.
22. Ibid., 280–81.
23. Ibid., 369–70.
24. Gerald Gunther, *Learned Hand: The Man and the Judge* (New York: Knopf, 1994), 548–49.
25. Richard Lovelace, "To Althea from Prison," M. H. Abrams, ed., *The Norton Anthology of English Literature, Revised,* vol. 1 (New York: W. W. Norton, 1968), 1204; the actual quote being, "Stone walls do not a prison make, nor iron bars a cage."